B. White and Son

Moral and Philosophical Estimates of the State and Faculties of Man

Vol. II

B. White and Son

Moral and Philosophical Estimates of the State and Faculties of Man
Vol. II

ISBN/EAN: 9783337070052

Printed in Europe, USA, Canada, Australia, Japan

Cover: Foto ©Thomas Meinert / pixelio.de

More available books at **www.hansebooks.com**

MORAL AND PHILOSOPHICAL

ESTIMATES

OF THE

STATE AND FACULTIES

OF

MAN;

AND OF THE

NATURE AND SOURCES

OF

HUMAN HAPPINESS.

A SERIES OF DIDACTIC LECTURES.

VOL. II.

LONDON,

PRINTED FOR B. WHITE AND SON, AT
HORACE'S HEAD, FLEET-STREET,
MDCCLXXXIX.

SECOND VOLUME.

a 2   XVIII.

ESTI-

ESTIMATE XI.

THE

VALUE

OF

SENSIBILITY.

And Jofeph faid unto his brethren, I am Jofeph;
—Doth my father yet live? And his brethren
could not anfwer him : for they were troubled
at his prefence.   And Jofeph faid unto his
brethren, Come near to me, I pray you ; and
they came near ; and he faid: I am Jofeph,—
your brother—whom ye fold into Ægypt.

Gen. xlv. 3, 4.

THE

VALUE

OF

SENSIBILITY.

THE teacher of religion muſt, like
all other teachers, apply himſelf to
the wants of his hearers and diſciples. He
muſt diſcourſe to them in that language
which is moſt intelligible to them; muſt
rectify ſuch of their opinions, as ſtand moſt
in need of it; and rouſe them from ſuch
faults as moſt frequently and moſt eaſily
gain the aſcendancy over them. And when
it happens that more is thought and ſpoken
of certain matters than uſual, and this in
words or expreſſions, the ſignification whereof is yet fluctuating and unſettled, he muſt

not

not let it efcape his attention, nor exclude it from his difcourfes and exhortations, whenever the fubject is of the moral kind, and has or may have an influence on the conduct and the happinefs of his hearers. Accordingly, Sirs, I take this to be the cafe with Senfibility ; of which we hear a great deal at prefent, and yet is a word much oftener ufed than rightly underftood. And, as this is a matter which may produce much good and much harm, occafion much happinefs and much mifery, I think I ftand in need of no farther excufe if I make an attempt to admonifh you on this matter, and to caution you againft the abufe of it.

In this defign I have read to you a paf-fage from the hiftory of Jofeph, wherein his character is depicted as abounding in fenfibility. The ftrongeft fentiments of love, and tendernefs, the nobleft generofity, fo overwhelm his foul, that he breaks out into tears, when he declares himfelf to his brethren.

brethren. All the eminence and fove-
reignty with which he was invefted, as the
deliverer of Ægypt, and the viceroy of its
king, could neither fupprefs nor weaken in
him the warmeft emotions of filial and
fraternal love, nor prevent the natural de-
monftrations of them. He felt the pure
and innocent delight a man enjoys in the
bofom of his family, the uncommon happinefs of finding loft friends again, and
the ftill greater felicity of forgiving the
injurious, of comforting the afflicted, and
of reftoring the difpirited to their former
vigour. And he preferred this pleafure,
and this happinefs, to all the fplendour and
all the luxuries afforded him by his prefent
elevated condition. "I am Jofeph, your
'brother. Doth my father yet live? Come
near to me. Now, be not grieved; nor
think that I am angry. God hath brought
this to pafs. It is he that hath done it all.
Oh happy me, that I am able to preferve
and provide for you, and yours!" Who

can

can here miftake the language of the heart, the moft generous, the moft fentimental heart!

But we are not to ftop here. Our defign is to confider the matter itfelf in all its latitude ; and, as far as may be done in fuch a difcourfe, fet it in a proper light. In this view we fhall have three queftions to difcufs.

The firft is, What is fenfibility ?

The fecond, What is true, generous, and laudable fenfibility ? And

The third, What is falfe and blameable fenfibility ?

For acquiring a juft idea of fenfibility, we muft take care not to confound it with fenfitivenefs, or fimply take them for one and the fame. When we are eafily af-
feﬔed

fected by the things we fee, and hear, and
feel; or by the reprefentations we form to
ourfelves of abfent, vifible, fpiritual fubjects; or by the images which our imagination or inventive faculty holds up to us,
of mere poffibilities or of actual exift-
ences; when the agreeable or difagreeable
impreffions which either of them make
upon us fink deep, and eafily and fuddenly
feize upon our whole fenfitive faculty,
eafily and fuddenly move us to joy or to
forrow, to weeping or to laughter, to love
or to hatred, to zeal or to anger, to tranfports of delight, or to the pungency of
affliction; we are then acutely fenfitive:
and, when this fenfitivenefs is ennobled and
exalted; when it chiefly difplays itfelf in
regard to moral objects, to more refined
beauties, and to fublimer pleafures; when
it fharpens our fentiments of what is right
and wrong, good and bad, becoming and
unbecoming, generous and ungenerous;
and makes us readily obferve and acutely

feel

feel this difference in such things, persons, actions, and events, wherein the generality of mankind perceive and feel nothing,— then are we sensible. A few antithetical exemplifications will set this matter in a more perspicuous light. The merely sensitive man is rather moved by the surface and the exterior of things; the man of sensibility more by their intrinsic qualities and real excellency. The former is in particular easily moved to displeasure and to anger; the other is adapted to all, and chiefly the gentler, nobler kinds of sentiments. The former is more agitated by strong and violent impressions; the latter more touched and affected by the milder and more gentle. The former is more sensible to the grand, the extraordinary, and the striking; the latter, more to the fine, the noble, the unobserved and despised beautiful and good. The sensitive man is irritated at the injury he receives or is offered; the man of sensibility is troubled like-

likewife on account of the injury his ene-
my is doing to himfelf, and the affliction
he is preparing for himfelf, fooner or later
to undergo. The fenfitive man is more
frequently moved to compaffion by the
loud complaints and the copious tears of
the unhappy; the man of fenfibility is alfo
affected by the filent expreffions of the
pain, the troubles, and the want which he
interefts himfelf in, in regard of every
creature. The fenfitive man loves rather
gay and noify pleafures and diverfions; the
man of fenfibility feeks moft the charms
of quiet, domeftic, gentle joys. The fenfitive man rejoices in the good actions of
the philanthropift and the patriot; the man
of fenfibility is likewife delighted in the
tears that ftand in the eyes of the child,
when he hears of noble deeds, which he
wifhes to have done himfelf. The fenfitive
man is full of feeling towards whatever
has a vifible and intimate influence on himfelf and his; the man of fenfibility is alfo

7   moved

moved by the remoter and more hidden confequences of things; and nothing is totally foreign to him, nothing indifferent, that relates to any living being capable of feeling and of happinefs. In fhort, fenfibility is enlarged, refined and generous fenfation; it is either a higher degree, a peculiar direction or difpofition, or a nobler ufe and exhibition of it.

Now, if fenfation be of itfelf a true and honourable prerogative of man, then fenfibility muft be as much fo and more. But, as the former may be fometimes rightly employed, fometimes abufed, and therefore fometimes ufeful, and at others hurtful, to mankind, fo likewife it fares with the latter. There is a real and a falfe, a laudable and a blameable, an innocent and a dangerous fenfibility. Let us fee wherein they both confift, and whereby they may be difcriminated from each other.

Our

Our fensibility is, in the first place, of the right kind, it is generous and respectable, when directed to the best and nobleft objects. There are undoubtedly certain objects that cannot make too strong an impreffion on us, which cannot too much affect us, which we cannot too deeply feel : and thefe are God, truth, innocence, virtue, human perfection, and happinefs; all that is beautiful, and great, and good, and honourable and amiable, and remaineth for ever. Therefore, if thou never thinkeft, O man! upon thy God, without the higheft reverence and filial love, as thy Creator and Father; if thou never confidereft his works without a chearful admiration, a genial enlargement of thy heart, and a lively fenfe of the traces of his wifdom, and goodnefs in the fmaller as well as the larger parts of his creation; if never without tranfport, thou lifteft up thine eyes to his magnificent heavens, or beholdeft the numberlefs beauties of the earth,

earth, which he hath appointed for t
dwelling; if, not without inward delig
thou enjoyeft his benefactions and bleffin
or reflecteft on his bounty and love; if, wl
thou feeft thy fellow-creatures, thy brethr
and walkeft and converfeft with them, tł
art not without a real intereft in them ;
thou art not deftitute of inward fatisfact
when thou art the witnefs of a good ;
generous deed, or obferveft the conquef
truth over error, and of virtue over vi
nor feeft the triumph of unrighteoufr
and iniquity without emotion, nor tyrai
of any kind without the livelieft difpleafi
nor fuffering or corrupted innocence wi
out deep concern; nor the perverfenefs ;
mifery of thy fellow-creatures without
tual forrow; if, when thou heareft
voice of nature, of truth, and of nc
fimplicity, thou art not without pleaf
and delight, or the cry of the indigent
without hearty compaffion, the fighs of
deftitute and afflicted not without pain

gr

grief; in short, when thou performest every act of private and public worship with a heart full of sentiment, prayest with real ardour, feelest the whole value and the whole dignity of thy connection with God and with his son Jesus Christ, art warmed and penetrated with love towards Jesus Christ, and thy devotions are replete with comforts and blessings which thy heart can scarcely contain; then is thy sensibility directed to objects and placed upon objects that are worthy of it; then is it of the nobleft kind, then does it turn to thy highest advantage, and is the source of perfection and happiness to thyself and to others, for the present and the future world.

Our sensibility is, farther, of the proper kind; it is blamelefs, and a real advantage to man, when constantly under the dominion and guidance of reason. Sentiment, and therefore likewise sensibility, cannot be a safe direction to us on all occasions. It is

apt

apt to bias us too eafily and too violently for or againft a matter or a perfon; frequently moves us too much where we ought to be firm and immoveable; it renders us too often, from indulgence and favour, to be lenient towards one unjuft perfon, and too fevere againft another; too often makes us tender towards the diftreffed from compaffion, and hard againft the fuccefsful. It judges too frequently with partiality; abides too obftinately by the firft impreffions made upon the heart; it allows itfelf to be cheated by the appearances of beautiful and good, by impofing pretences, by moving words and geftures. And, befides, how many men are there who regard this refpectable quality as weaknefs, and treat it accordingly, and are expert in taking advantage of it by a thoufand different means, and making it ferve their difhoneft purpofes! How neceffary is it, then, that it fhould be conftantly under the controul of reafon, that it fhould have a

clear

clear well-regulated underſtanding for its
guide, if it would not be continually falling
into error, if we would have it not more
hurtful than profitable to ourſelves and to
others! How many perſons of ſenſibility
have thereby brought miſery on themſelves
and others, or plunged themſelves into no
ſmall ſtraights and difficulties, by not
hearkening to the admonitions and remon-
ſtrances of this conductor, and diſcarding
reaſon with contempt as being too cold, too
tedious, too intereſted a counſellor and
guide! No; this muſt be the ruler of our
ſoul, the director of our conduct; to this
end the Creator hath beſtowed it upon us,
and it is the true, the great prerogative of
man, as a rational creature. It is this that
muſt diſcriminate ſemblance from truth,
that muſt teach us to ſacrifice even our beſt
deſires to the performance of duty, to act,
not according to fortuitous and extrava-
gant ſentiments, but upon firm and im-
mutable principles, and to controul and
govern

govern ourfelves, though the conflict coft
never fo much to our heart. Happy the
man, who is thus taught of reafon ; whofe
effential character is compofed of light and
warmth, whofe underftanding is as enlightened as his heart is fenfible !

In fhort, our fenfibility is of the proper
kind, it is innocent and refpectable, when
it renders us active in doing good, when it
incites to the beft and moft generous actions.
To feel, to feel acutely, and not properly
to manage our feelings, in general betrays
weaknefs and effeminacy. To be fenfible
to goodnefs, and yet not perform that good,
when we can and ought, is inconfiftency
and hypocrify. To be fatisfied with having
good fentiments, inftead of doing good actions, is impofture and felf-deceit. The
feweft emotions we have are ultimate objects ; the generality are and muft be no
more than means, inducements, and incitements, to put us upon action, and to facilitate

litate the application and exertion of our faculties, and to affift us in the overcoming of many difficulties and dangers. What is the moft enraptured admiration of the beautiful and the good, if it do not raufe us to the imitation of it? What is the moft pungent compaffion, if it do not ex-cite us to actual and immediate relief? What is the moft extreme difpleafure, the moft ardent zeal, when it does not carry us to the prevention of injuftice, to the defence of the oppreffed, to a ftedfaft fup-port of the caufe of truth, and to add courage and ftrength to the innocent? Of what ufe are fighs, and tears, and lamenta-tions, if, when we ought to be acting and working, affifting others by counfel or deeds, they leave us irrefolute and motion-lefs? What is the moft paffionate and hearty affection, unlefs it fhew itfelf by actions? No; if we would have our fen-fibility of the proper kind, forwarded and improved by virtue, then we muft not fo

VOL. II. C far

far furrender ourfelves up to it, as to let
it exhauft our faculties, and deprive us of
the power to act. No; it muft much
rather impel us by an irrefiftible force to
all good and generous atchievements; and
put away all confiderations which might
withhold us from them; fecure us from
any hurtful delay; overcome every difpofition to floth and eafe; fortify us againft
every dread of difficulty and danger; and
prompt us to well doing with as much zeal,
as we have deeply felt the propriety of it;
and the more active it renders us in thefe
refpects, the more refpectable and honourable it is.

And this, Sirs, this is real, irreproachable, virtuous fenfibility; which no man,
who has a right turn of mind, and whofe
heart is not totally hardened, will venture
to blame or to defpife; which every man,
who knows the value of things, muft revere
as a precious gift of the Moft High, as a
                                          real

real prerogative of man. The cafe is quite otherwife with falfe fenfibility. We need only to examine it a little for difcovering it to be blameable and hurtful.

Senfibility is, in the firft place, falfe, and blameable, when it is not natural, but forced; when a man expreffes and pretends to feelings which he has not, or ftrives to appear to have them in a far higher degree than he actually has : thus playing the part of a defperate, a perfectly inconfolable man, when he is only moderately troubled and grieved ; or falfely pretending to enjoy a heavenly tranfport and rapturous delight, when he only receives an ordinary pleafure and a calm fatisfaction in any particular thing. Nay, our fenfations do not always depend upon ourfelves, are not always in our power ; no man, in every inftant of his life, and in every temperament of his body, is alike capable of the fame degree of fenfibility; neither mind nor body is always

able

able to endure an equally ftrong tenfion
and vibration : fo that none need be
afhamed either of a deficiency of thefe
ftronger fenfations, or of the accidental re-
laxation of them. Indeed, he that is always infenfible, always unfeeling, whom
nothing can move, is in no defirable condition; and is criminal, if he has brought
himfelf into it by folly and vice : yet likewife the moft fenfible man is not always
alike conftituted ; and the greateft wonders
of the works of nature do not always
ftrike his view in the fame manner ; even
upon the tendereft heart, reprefentations of
the indigence and mifery of a fellow-
creature do not always make the fame impreffion. Whoever but approves the true,
the beautiful, the good, and does that
which he reckons his duty, need never be
grieved if he perform it at times, 'as it
were, though readily and chearfully, yet
without any remarkably ftrong fenfation,
with fedatenefs and diligence. Whereas
　　　　　　　　　　　　　　　　he

he that will exhibit the fame fenfations in
every event, and is refolved to feel in one
circumftance in the fame manner and degree as in another, for the fake of being
reckoned a man of extraordinary fenfibility, among thofe with whom he is intimately connected by a uniformity of fentiments and purfuits, muft frequently act
the hypocrite, muft often lie, muft often
fpeak and act in an unnatural manner:
and no kind of diffimulation and conftraint
more eafily betrays itfelf, none makes a
more difagreeable impreffion on thofe that
fee it and hear it, than this. Senfations
totally incompatible will frequently be exhibited at the fame time; frequently the
aid of the moft contradictory geftures and
motions of the body will be called in ; frequently all the energetical and moving expreffions of language will be heaped on
one another without judgement or choice ;
and many performances of this nature end
in the fneers and derifion of the fpectators.

C 3   Farther,

Farther, fenfibility is falfe and blameable, when it is overftrained or exceffive; when it is difproportionate to the value of the object; when it is more difplayed in trifles than in matters of importance. Many will hear the account of the demolition of a whole city by the horrors of an earthquake, of a fleet dafhed to pieces upon rocks, of an army deftroyed by fire and fword, with all the indifferency imaginable, who can fhed tears over a comparatively infignificant creature of the claffes of plants or animals. On numbers, a whole life fpent in toil-fome, virtuous actions, but performed in filence, without any rumour or report, makes no impreffion, who will fall into tranfports and extafy at an act of humanity or beneficence, accidentally perhaps performed by another, but done with great fhow, and difplayed with much oftentation. Many are fcarcely moved, or even not at all, by indications of courage, fortitude of mind, refolution, invincible patience and

firm-

firmnefs; while, at any thing that fhews
tendernefs or love, even though it be not
perfectly innocent, they find reafon to be
moved in the higheft degree. The man of
fenfibility, in the beft and nobleft fenfe of
the word, finds indeed matter for his fenfibility to work upon in a thoufand events
and fubjects, where others would be abfolutely cold, which in their eyes would be
infignificant trifles; and it deferves no re-
proach when a flower or a little infect
moves him, when he obferves any expreffion of exultation or fuffering in any fenfitive creature, that he is affected by it, and
partakes of it all with a fentimental heart:
but he does not therefore overlook great
and important concernments, is not cold
towards them, takes ftill more intereft
in them, will be ftill more ftrongly affected by them, does not fall into the
ridiculous, but conftantly preferves the
dignity of a thinking, rational, and felf-
poffeffing man; and this it is that fhews

C 4

his

his way of thinking and feeling to be no artificial fentimentality, but true and generous fenfibility.

Senfibility is, in the third place, illegitimate and blameable, when it is hurtful or dangerous to ourfelves and others; hinders us in our actual duties, or renders the performance of them difagreeable and difficult; when it deprives us of the defire and the ability to do what is right and good. He that fuffers himfelf to be moved and overcome by the expreffion of violent pain, by the fight of fufferings and mifery, as to be put befide himfelf, to lofe his power of reflection and prefence of mind, and renders himfelf incapable of attending to the means, and to the application of the means by which pain may be eafed, thofe fufferings mitigated, that mifery removed or affuaged; he that weeps and laments, where he ought and may relieve; his fenfibility is hurtful and reproachable; and,

though

though it be never fo natural, is the ficknefs of the foul, and the infirmity of the
mind, which can never acquire the man
any praife, which he ought not to cherifh
and maintain, but fhould labour to guard
himfelf againft, with all poffible care.

Senfibility is, again, hurtful, and confe-
quently criminal, when it renders us negligent in our behaviour towards others,
and forgetful of the duties we owe them ;
when it deprives us of the relifh for our
ordinary affairs, takes us off from the profecution of them, or tempts us to floth,
and to regard them with diflike and aver-
fion. It is therefore hurtful, when a mif-
trefs of a family allows it to be a hindrance
to her in the careful attendance on her
domeftic employment, in the maintenance
of regularity and order in all the parts of
it, in her diligent endeavours to promote
the welfare and fatisfaction of her family,
in her attention to fmall things as well as

to

to great; when fhe chufes rather to indulge her fenfibility in reading, or in converfing with fentimental acquaintances, than addict herfelf to domeftic and œconomical affairs; or will only extend her influence and infpection in general over the whole, as if that could fubfift without its parts, and the greater without the lefs.

Senfibility is hurtful and criminal, when the young man, or the man of bufinefs, is induced by it to think the concerns of his trade or vocation unworthy of him, and which perhaps are not very elegant and important in themfelves, or not highly entertaining, and thereupon to defpife and neglect them, and to imagine that he degrades himfelf by paying attention to them, and by doing only fuch things as a thoufand others of lefs delicate fentiments, and of a lefs elevated mind, can perform as well as he. It is hurtful, when the difciple of wifdom is feduced by this propenfity of

his

his heart to neglect the due cultivation of his underſtanding and reaſon, and to refuſe himſelf to ſerious and dry ſtudies, though of the higheſt importance for acquiring the knowledge and the ſciences, which are indiſpenſably neceſſary to his future pro-feſſion or ſtation in life.

Senſibility is hurtful and criminal when it leads a man to refrain from aſſociating with others, from the duties of converſa-tion, company, friendly eſteem and love, becauſe they are not ſo ſentimental as him-ſelf; nature having probably formed them of groſſer materials, or addicted them more to cool and temperate reflection, given them more conſideration, and diſpoſed them more to action than to ſentiment.

Laſtly, ſenſibility is hurtful and dan-gerous, when it induces us, by its inſpira-tions and impulſes, to dream of a world, and to live and float in a world, which has
hardly

hardly any thing in common with the actual
ftate of things, which exifts only in our
imagination, or in certain poems and works
of fancy; when we are feduced, by fuch
reprefentations and images, to look for
perfection in others, and to expect matters
from them, which are either never, or
very rarely, to be found; and then to
trouble and afflict ourfelves at this natural
defect, and to keep ourfelves at a diftance
from them, as if we were effential fufferers
by them. How many has this kept from
making the moft fuitable and moft advantageous connections! how many has it
forced to pafs their days in a ftate of celi-
bacy! how many have thereby become
bad hufbands, felfifh, and auftere, companions hard to be pleafed, and downright
mifanthropifts! No; the wife man fees,
accepts, and ufes the things of this world
as they are, and looks for no angels among
mankind, no paradife upon the earth, no
perfect virtue among frail and finful crea-

I   tures,

tures, no perfection there, where it is not to be found.

No; in all thefe cafes where we have pronounced fenfibility to be hurtful and criminal, we facrifice obligations to pleafure; render ourfelves indifpofed and unfit for the performance of our duty; perform it negligently; deftroy the harmony and welfare of focial life; act againft the defigns of God and our own nature, by which we are ordained, not only to feel, but alfo to think, and, ftill more, to act; we enervate our tafte and our heart; weaken our faculties; become faftidious in the enjoyment of the beautiful and the good; feldom fatisfied with what is and what has been; and prepare for ourfelves and others a thoufand fufferings and a thoufand woes, from which the man in contrary cafes would be abfolutely free.

Guard

Guard yourfelves, therefore, Sirs, from this falfe, exceffive, and hurtful fenfibility. Let moderation and prudence be the guides of your heart. And, as you are chriftians, in this refpect look likewife to Jefus, your conductor and chief, the pattern of all human perfection. How full of feeling was his heart; and how generous, how bufied, was his fenfibility; how fruitful in good works! Whofe foul was ever fo thoroughly imbued with love towards God and man, with the love of truth and virtue, as his! What harmony of mind and heart, of words and works! He lamented over the people; he compaffionated their fpiritual and perfonal wants; but at the fame time he gave them effectual relief; he filled and inftructed them. He wept when he faw his friend Lazarus in the grave; but he awakened him from the dead. He felt and fuffered the ficknefs and pains of the wretched, and healed them. He ca-
reffed

reffed the little children that they brought
unto him, and gave them his prayers. He
viewed the young man who wanted to follow him, with affection and love, though
his wifhes were not brought to effect. He
fhed tears over Jerufalem, while it was
watching his motions with a murderous
intent. He prayed for pardon for his tor-
mentors; and forgot himfelf whenever he
had an opportunity of ferving and helping
others. And what a concern he took in
the welfare of his relations in the moft ca-
lamitous moment of his life! " Behold,"
faid he from the crofs to his favourite
difciple, " Behold thy mother!" And to
Mary, " Behold thy fon!"—But how active
was his whole life in all thefe refpects!
How unremitted his zeal in righteoufnefs
and beneficence, in finifhing the work that
was given him to do! How clear and unclouded his intellect! How impartial his
judgement! How unfhaken his fortitude!
How

How juft and folid his principles! How
great his indulgence to his difciples and
fcholars, who were fo much lefs fenfible
than he; who feemed at times almoft totally void of feeling! How manly, in
fhort, was his whole difcourfe, and his
whole behaviour! How far from all conftraint, all artifice, and all oftentation!
How adapted to his character, his vocation, and to temporary circumftances!
What noifelefs and tranquil dignity he difplayed, in all he uttered, and in all he
did!

Oh imitate him likewife in this, all ye
who have the happinefs and the honour to
be his confeffors. Strive after the perfection of your nature with all the faculties of your foul. Attend to your underftanding as well as to your heart. Cultivate it with no lefs care. Learn to think
juftly as well as to feel forcibly. Let
your

your reafon and your fenfibility go hand
in hand along the path of life. Let this
be governed and directed by that, and
that be encouraged and animated by this.
Thus, you will neither be deficient in light,
for avoiding all deviation and error ; nor
in warmth and force, for purfuing the right
way, refolute and indefatigable.

ESTIMATE XII.

THE

VALUE

OF

VIRTUE.

Wisdom is better than rubies; and all the things that may be desired are not to be compared to it.

Prov. viii. 11.

THE

VALUE

OF

VIRTUE.

TO defpife virtue, and not to prize it enough, are two very different matters. The former is a fault, of which only a few are capable; the latter is a failing, of which great numbers of perfons render themfelves guilty. Virtue, Sirs, is of fo harmlefs, fo venerable, and fo captivating an afpect; fhe leaves us fo little to fear, and allows us to hope for fo much from thofe with whom we perceive her, and by whom we fee her act and operate; her fentiments and her conduct are fo juft,

fo

ſo harmonious, ſo natural, and ſimple; her
connection with our happineſs, and with
the welfare of the whole community, is in
moſt caſes, at leaſt in many, ſo apparent;
ſhe is frequently ſo indiſpenſably neceſſary,
is conſtantly ſo beautiful, holds out ſo much
indulgence and patience to the frail and
feeble; that neither perſpicacity, nor erudition, nor habitual reflection, nor a higher
degree of perſonal perfection, are requi-
ſite for allowing her a certain value, for
acknowledging her to be ſomething good
and reſpectable, and for ſhewing her more
or leſs eſteem. The wiſe and the ignorant,
the good and the bad, the virtuous and
the vicious, the conſiderate man and the
thoughtleſs youth, are all of one accord in
this general judgement on the value of
virtue; and none will venture, unleſs he
be under the deceitful influence of ſome
violent paſſion, plainly and in direct terms
to deſpiſe her. Wherever conſcience,
wherever the ſentiment of truth and goodneſs

nefs ftill remains in man, there virtue finds
an advocate in the hearts of her enemies
as well as of her friends, which dares not
venture plainly to condemn her.

But, certain as this is, it is no lefs certain, that all men do not, that probably
only the leaft part of mankind acknowledge the whole value of virtue, and fo
highly prize, and fo inwardly revere her,
as fhe deferves.   The reverence fhewn to
virtue is with great numbers more prejudice, or obfcure fenfation, than vital reflected knowledge, real fentiment, or firm
internal conviction.   They have a refpect
for virtue at large and in general; but not
as it appears in every particular incident,
and every particular perfon.   They hold it,
indeed, to be fomething good and defirable;
but they feldom give it the decided preference to all other good and defirable
things, after mature confideration, and by
particular tokens.   But feldom are we per-
D 4   fuaded

fuaded by fincere conviction, that we muft not part with it on any account, that we cannot purchafe it at too dear a rate, nor make too great facrifices to it; that with it we poffefs all things, and without it nothing; that it is infinitely better to be poor, and mean, unlearned and defpifed, but virtuous, than to be rich and mighty, confidered and learned, but not virtuous. And all our pretences to real virtue are idle and bafelefs, fo long as we do not believe and confefs this truth, fo long as we do not prefer it before every other advantage of life, however eftimable and excellent.

To fettle your judgement on this matter, Sirs, and to increafe your reverence for virtue, is the defign of my prefent difcourfe. In feveral foregoing difcourfes we have laid before you the value of riches, of honour, of fenfual pleafures, and of fpiritual pleafures; pronounced them all, fo far as they are real, to be actual goods,

to

to be objects which, in a certain degree, deserve to be esteemed, admired, fought after, and enjoyed; to be things, which, according to the use we make of them, may contribute more or less to our perfection and happiness. Useful and valuable, however, as all these things may be, virtue is still far preferable to them, as far as the end is to the means, and as a stately edifice is preferable to the scaffoldings and implements that are necessary to its construction.

Wisdom, says the wise king in the Bible, wisdom is better than rubies, and all the things that may be desired are not to be compared to it. Wisdom, in this passage, is not barely that which men usually call understanding, knowledge, erudition, or profound penetration. It is the proper use of the understanding in all the affairs and transactions of mankind; the right application of the knowledge and sagacity we possess, to the promoting of our felicity;

2   it

it is an intelligent conduct in harmony with truth and order; in fhort, it is, in fignification, exactly the fame as what we imply by the word Virtue. This wifdom, this virtue, is more precious than rubies; all that we can poffibly defire is not to be compared to it; that is, it's value is fuperior to the value of all other things which ufually men paffionately defire, and moft earneftly ftrive to obtain.

And this is the matter we fhall now endeavour circumftantially to elucidate, and prove to demonftration.

In this defign we have two queftions to anfwer.

The firft, What is Virtue?

The fecond, Whence does it acquire its pre-eminent value?

Virtue

Virtue does not confift in particular good
actions. Neither temperance, nor chaftity,
nor juftice, nor equity, nor beneficence,
give us the idea of what virtue is, and
what it implies. Thefe are no more than
the feveral ways in which it is difplayed,
the effects of its operation. It is the foundation, the fource of thefe and all other
good actions. That the eye fees without
obftruction, that the ear without difficulty
hears, that every natural fenfe imbibes the
impreffion of outward things, that every
limb and member of the body performs its
functions with regularity and eafe, is not
what is meant by the effential of health;
they are only the various effects and indications of it. Health confifts in the juft
and proper relation of all the parts, all the
veffels and juices of our whole body with
one another, and in the undebilitated freedom of action of the vital powers which
pervade, and cherifh, and fet them all in
motion.

Virtue,

Virtue, in like manner, does not confift in particular good difpofitions. That we find a pleafure in beneficence; that we intenfely reflect on ferious fubjects; that we heartily promote peace and concord; that we are more difpofed to think well than ill of our fellow-creatures: thefe are all good difpofitions, in which the virtuous perfon cannot be deficient; but none of thefe difpofitions alone, nor even feveral of them together, render us truly virtuous, or form the diftinction, the effential of true virtue.

No; virtue is an aggregate, an indivifible whole. It is not fo much action, as principle of action; not fo much fentiment, as principle of fentiment. It impels us to thofe good actions, and infpires us with thefe good fentiments. Animated and governed by it, we will and do what is good; we incline to it with energy and decifion, and practife it heartily and firmly. It is, in effect, the frame of our fpirit, the direction

rection and application of our faculties,
which prompts us conftantly to think, to
be inclined, and to act, in conformity to
truth, to regularity, and to the will of
God. It confifts in a general, prevalent,
effective defire after whatever is true, and
right, and good, proportionate to our nature and our relative fituations, and the
nature and relations of other things, in the
conftant readinefs to do or not to do, to
fuffer or to bear, to be and to have, what
God will have us to do or not to do, to
bear or to fuffer, to be and to have, or not
to be and not to have. It confifts in the
truth of our reflections, feelings, defires,
our words and works, in the harmony of
every part of our inward and outward conduct, among themfelves, and with the law
of God. It is therefore precifely what we
commonly term the love and practice of
goodnefs, a ready and unlimited obedience
towards God and his commandments, or
univerfal righteoufnefs. It is the health
and

and the true life of the foul, the ftate of
our fpirit, when it is and does what it
ought to be and to do, according to its
proper ordination ; the force which conftantly impels us to all that is fair and
good, and generous and ufeful, what is
agreeable to God, and promotes the perfection and happinefs of man,—replenifhes
us with good-will to all men, and induces
us to live and act more for others than for
ourfelves, and to employ whatever we are
and have in the moft ufeful manner.

Now, fuch a virtue, we may repeat it,
is of more value than all the other goods,
the value whereof we have hitherto confidered and fettled in feveral difcourfes ; of
more value than riches, than honour, than
the pleafures of the fenfes, more than all
the advantages and pleafures of the fpirit,
as they are at variance with virtue, or in-
dependent thereon. The following remarks
will

will fet this in its proper light, and render it evident.

First, Virtue is purely, and without all limitation, good; purely, and without all limitation or exception, ufeful and honourable. This we cannot pronounce of any other good; though in itfelf, and under certain conditions, never fo eftimable. Riches may be a fnare to us, and honours a burden: fenfible pleafures may become a fource of trouble and pain; they all may lead us into fin and vice, and thereby plunge us into mifery. Even the diftinctions of the mind, knowledge and fcience, wit and penetration, and the fublimer pleafures they produce, may be mifapplied in a thoufand ways, and in a thoufand ways become hurtful and deftructive to ourfelves and others. Neither outward wealth nor faculties of mind can fhield the ignorant and vicious from folly and mifery. Virtue alone can never be mifapplied, can never

be

be criminal : for a man cannot be too virtuous; cannot be too faithful, too juft, or
think and act too well ; nor enjoy the pleafures of virtue too often and too conftantly, nor by that enjoyment grow negligent
of his duties. No one virtue is at variance
with any other ; none is an impediment to
the practice of another ; none leffens our
defire or weakens our faculties for another.
Properly there is but one virtue (as I have
already obferved), and that is, the predominant, unchangeable readinefs to do that
which is lawful and right, and is the beft
in every cafe, whatever is in conformity
with nature, with the will of God, with
our relationfhip to him and other things.
And wherever the readinefs and aptitude
is, there no contention, no contradiction
with itfelf, can find place, no duty to be
obferved to the difadvantage or neglect of
another, no kind of moral good to be
fought and exhibited at the expence of
another.

The

The value of virtue is likewife, in the fecond place, far more unchangeable than the value of all other goods and advantages. The value of riches will be regulated according to our wants, and the wants of the fociety in which we live. We may fuppofe cafes, where they are totally ufelefs, and become a mere burden to us. The value of honour changes according to the opinions, the ufages, and the political eftablifhments of mankind; it rifes and falls, and becomes in itfelf more or lefs refpectable, according as the outward tokens of general eftimation are more rare or more numerous, are diftributed with difcreet felection, or indifcriminately conferred : and out of focial life, in the filence of retirement, they almoft ceafe to be diftinctions. The value of pleafure is not more fixed and permanent : how dependent is it on events, on derived and received opinions, and tacit agreements and fecret convention ! how much on the formation of our body, the

difpofition of our nerves, the ftate of our
health, our age, and other circumftances!
how various and how different the afpects
under which it appears in different times
and different places! how often is it in-
fipid, how often irkfome, how often does
it ceafe from being pleafure, and how frequently it changes into pain! Even the
advantages of the mind, underftanding,
erudition, knowledge, and art, are liable
to numberlefs alterations. Their value
changes according to the prevailing tafte;
as this or the other kind of fcience or
mental exertions are more or lefs efteemed,
admired, and preferred.

The value of virtue alone is always im-
mutable; at all times, among all nations,
in all circumftances, amidft the manifold
changes and chances of life, alone unchangeable. Indeed, not that which we
peculiarly call virtue, which may be differently eftimated in different times and
placess,

placcs, may be fometimes of greater and fometimes of fmaller worth. But the way of thinking and acting, the difpofition of mind, the character, the ftate of a rational being, which we term virtue, and which alone deferves that name, are and remain for ever the fame, always and every where retain their value. Truth, order, goodnefs, integrity, can never ceafe from being truth, order, goodnefs, and integrity, though we live in this place or in that, are connected with thefe or with other men, in folitude or in fociety, in profperity or in adverfity, in health or in ficknefs. Even after our terreftrial life, they are and remain exactly what they were in themfelves. Riches, honour, and pleafure, are totally loft to us in death. We cannot even refcue all mental pleafures from deftruction. Who knows how much or how little of our knowledge, our fcience, or our art, and of the pleafures that attend them, we fhall be able to take with us into the other world? All

that

that we now reckon for fuch we certainly
fhall not retain.—But nothing, Sirs, nothing
can attack our virtue; nothing diminifh its
value. The regularity that has once got
the fway of our foul, the good qualities it
has once acquired, its love towards all that
is true and good, its love to God and man,
remain with it after the death of the body,
as certainly as it retains them till that death
arrive. They will be of exactly the fame
value in the future ftate as in the prefent,—
will be then precifely as perfect, as bleffed,
and render the foul far more perfect and
more bleffed, than they could do here.

The value of virtue is, in the third
place, much more univerfal and indepen-
dent on ftation and connection than that of
all other, and particularly of outward
things; or, it is more univerfally ufeful
than all others, and therefore poffeffes a
greater worth than they. Riches would
utterly ceafe to be riches, if all men lived
in

in abundance. Honour would lose much
of its value, at least in the present state of
things, if it gave us no precedence over
others; if every man could make the same
pretenfions to it, and produce his authentic
claims. Many kinds of pleafure muft lofe
their title to that name, if all men could
partake in the enjoyment of them; many
others would be far lefs prized and fought
after, if they were not, in fome degree, the
property of certain states and conditions of
men. Society in general could not fubfift,
if the enjoyment of all the pleafures of the
fenfes, even the moft innocent of them,
and all the means and opportunities of it,
were alike free to every man. Even as
little could human fociety fubfift, if all the
members of it purfued only mental pleafures, if they were only to exercife themfelves in fcientific attainments, or in divert-
ing and amufing knowledge; and a great
proportion of the value of thefe things
would prefently be reduced to nothing, if

E 3 every

every man possessed them, and every man in the same degree.

Quite otherwise is the case with virtue. That is, and remains, among all classes and conditions of men, the same. It accommodates itself to every rank, to every calling; and to every occupation of life. It elevates every rank, dignifies every calling, and alleviates every occupation of life. It adapts itself to both high and low, to the rich and the poor, to the learned and the unlearned, to every age, to both sexes, to all societies. It is profitable and honourable to all. It loosens no band of social life; but ties them all closer together. No man loses any thing by it, if another be virtuous likewise : but if all were virtuous, all would profit, infinitely profit thereby. Neither can virtue be too prevalent or too common, or have too much influence on the dispositions and conduct of mankind. The more virtue, the less discord

cord and mifery! the more virtue, the more peace and felicity!

Virtue has, fourthly, a fuper-eminent value, by the excellent effects it produces in us; by the extraordinary influence it has on our perfection and happinefs. It makes us much better, much more ufeful to our fellow-creatures, much fitter for a fuperior life, much more clofely allied to God, than any other privilege or advantage we poffefs.

Virtue renders us much better. Riches, honour, fenfible and fpiritual pleafures, may ameliorate our outward condition, procure us agreeable fenfations; may fur-nifh us with incitements, means, oppor-tunity for acquiring found knowledge, for the practice of good works, and for pro-moting our moral amendment. Virtue is the thing performed by all thefe means, the end and aim to which they all con-

duce;

duce; it brings this amendment to effect, and makes us actually as perfect as our nature allows. Or, what is perfection but the harmony and full confent of all the parts to one ultimate end and aim, the beſt ſtate to which any thing is capable of being brought? And is not virtue this? Does not the moſt beautiful order and harmony prevail in the ſoul of the virtuous man? Are not all his defires and powers directed to what is true and good? Is he not continually aiming at the ſelf-ſame mark? Has he not the ſame unalterable view in all he thinks, and wills, and does?

Virtue makes us far more generally uſe-ful than the poſſeſſion of any other pre-rogative. Riches, honour, ſcience, and knowledge, are no more than means of diverſified beneficence; means of becoming uſeful to our fellow-creatures in a high degree. But, ſo long as virtue does not accompany and guide us in the applica-

2   tion

tion of thefe means, fo long fhall we comparatively perform but little by them; we
fhall be often weary of employing them to
that end; fhall frequently do harm by
them inftead of good. It is virtue that
teaches us rightly to ufe all thefe advantages, to employ them in the beft and
nobleft manner. Riches, honour, art, and
fcience, are commonly hurtful without
virtue; are very often the food and implements of the moft deftructive paffions.
But virtue, without riches, without honour,
without art and fcience, is and remains ftill
ufeful; ftill performs much good, much
pure and unalloyed good. Even the
pooreft, the loweft, the moft unlearned
man, if he has but virtue, may perform
unnumbered acts of goodnefs, according
to the extent of the fphere in which he
moves. How much may he do by advice,
by deed, by confolation, and by example!
And how much more extenfively, how
much more powerfully, may he operate,

if

if he be adorned and embellifhed by thofe advantages, and ftill retain his virtue!

Virtue likewife renders us more happy than any thing elfe can do. Riches and honour, indeed, procure us advantage; fenfible and mental pleafure afford us pleafing fenfations. But neither one nor the other can we enjoy fo frequently, and but feldom in fo high a degree, as we could defire. Both the one and the other may become ufelefs and prejudicial to us in a greater or lefs degree; may turn more to our difquiet than to our joy. Virtue alone can never become burdenfome, or ufelefs, or unneceffary to us. It bleffes us for ever; folaces, comforts, and rejoices us for ever; ever gives us the beft counfel; ever guides us the fureft way; ever brings us nearer to our aim. Where truth and order is, there is ferenity and fatisfaction : where pure and generous love prevails, there happinefs has fixt her throne. The man who

feels

feels and maintains his intrinsic dignity, can generally see himself stripped of all outward appendages, without becoming un- happy : the man whose will is in perfect consonance with the will of God, has and can do what he will, since he wills and does nothing but what God calls him to will and to do !

For the very same reason, virtue renders us fitter for a better and a higher life, than all other possessions; nay, that alone can render us capable of it. It passes for as much in heaven as it does upon earth, and much more. We are there as little liable to be deprived of it, as here. It is there the dignity and the life of our spirit, as well as here. Nay, there it is all in all; the most complete compensation for all the advantages we lose by death, the founda- tion of all greater and nobler activity, of all higher honour and power, the band of union between the inhabitants of the better world.

world. It is that which all the wife and good fubjects of God, in his whole immeafurable kingdom, have in common with each other; what indiffolubly binds them together, and intimately connects them with him, their Creator and Father.

Nay, virtue gives us a far greater refemblance to God than any advantage befide. What we call riches, is poverty with God. Our exaltation and power is the weaknefs and imbecillity of an infant in his eyes. Our very knowledge and erudition is, for the moft part, error and obfcurity in his purer light. By fuch advantages we acquire no likenefs to him, or only in an infinitely remote degree. But, to will what God wills; to love truth and order, as God loves them; to wifh well and to do good to all mankind, as he is benevolent and beneficent; to feek and find our fatisfaction in the beft employment of our faculties and the moft ufeful activity, as God finds

his

his therein : by thefe means we continually are approaching nearer to God—very
near—are continually becoming more like
him, and ever fitter for fellowfhip with
him. And it is virtue that exalts us to
this fimilitude, and virtue alone.

Who then can ftill entertain a doubt,
that it is the greateft and moft exalted of
all advantages, of all the kinds of property
we can poffefs, the beft and the moft defirable,—that it is of more value than
riches and honours, than ftation or power,
than pleafure, erudition, and fcience—more
than tranfient, quickly rifing and quickly
evaporating, devotion—more than health
and life ; virtue, which is the health of the
foul, and the life of the fpirit ?

It is likewife more valuable with God,
the centre of all virtue, than all things
elfe can be. It is the faireft lineament of
his likenefs in man ; the fole means whereby

by he can refemble him; the only privilege which God, by his meffengers, hath
honoured with his exprefs and fupreme
regard; the rule by which he will hereafter confer his glorious rewards on man.
If unaccompanied by virtue, he rejects the
moft coftly offerings, the moft folemn devotions, the moft auftere obfervances. With
it, he favourably accepts every good wifh
of the heart, every readinefs of the will,
every earneft endeavour.—It was virtue that
exalted an Abraham to be his peculiar
friend : it was fhe that affixed the mark of
the offspring of God on all the wife and
good of every age and clime. It was
fhe,—this daughter of heaven—that im-
preffed our Jefus with the ftamp of the
only-begotten, and the favourite of the
Father, as the fublimeft pattern of all
human perfection, rendered him capable
of the clofeft and moft intimate communion with God, and exalted him to be
Lord over all !

And

And canſt thou refuſe her thy eſteem,
O man! thy reverence, O chriſtian! who
haſt yet any ſentiment of what is venerable
and excellent! No; beware of ſtifling this
ſentiment of truth in thy heart! Let virtue
be the object of thy eſteem and reverence,
more than any thing that has hitherto de-
manded them of thee. In honouring virtue, thou honoureſt God. Eſteem and revere her, then, wherever thou findeſt her,
under whatever aſpect, in whatever garb,
ſhe appears, in what language ſoever ſhe
ſpeaks to thee, by what actions ſoever ſhe
makes herſelf known! Let not your love
of her be ſhewn only in general, but in
every particular perſon whom ſhe animates
and governs. Virtue, in the general, is no
more than an idea, a repreſentation of our
mind : ſhe actually exiſts only in particular
beings. In theſe we muſt eſteem and revere her. He that deſpiſes any poor and
low but virtuous man, deſpiſes virtue herſelf.

felf. And, if thou defpifeft virtue, O man! thou defpifeft all that is beautiful, and great, and venerable; thou defpifeft God, the fountain of all perfection.

But doft thou efteem her as fhe deferves? Oh then hefitate not a moment, what thou haft to do, which thou haft to chufe, when thou haft to determine between her and riches, between her and the honour of men, between her and fenfible or mental pleafures. Rather let them all be loft to thee, than forfake or violate her. Doft thou ftill refufe to facrifice all that militates with her? Doft thou ftill make anxious efforts to lofe nothing on either hand? Does any inconfiderable lofs, thou fuffereft for her fake, ftill give thee pain? Oh then, fay not that thou art virtuous!

No; Wilt thou be fo? Be fo without referve. Think not to put afunder what
God

God and the nature of things have joined
in the clofeft and moft indiffoluble bands.
Here at leaft we may fay with propriety,
All or nothing! No compofition can be
made in this matter!—So long as thou en-
deavoureft to affimilate and connect virtue
with vice—the two moft contradictory and
incompatible things in nature—with one
another, thou art doubly wretched. Thou
enjoyeft not the happinefs of virtue, and
thou only in part enjoyeft the fleeting and
tranfient pleafures of vice, not with a tranquil mind, not without fecret anguifh and
remorfe. Wouldft thou be happy, and
continually be adding to thy happinefs?
Oh, then, determine totally, and firmly,
and irrevocably, for Virtue! Let her inform and animate thy foul, convert thee,
as it were, into a new creature; let her be
thy guide and conductrefs in all times and
in all places; the moving fpirit of thy
whole behaviour! Then wilt thou fee

and

and experience how great, how unſpeak-
ably great, her value is; what dignity and
ſtrength ſhe imparts to man, what ſere-
nity and happineſs ſhe procures him; and
then wilt thou ſecure to thyſelf the poſſeſſion of her for ever and ever!

ESTI.

ESTIMATE XIII.

THE
SUPERIOR VALUE
OF
CHRISTIAN VIRTUE.

According as his divine power hath given unto us all things that pertain unto life and godliness, through the knowledge of him that hath called us to glory and virtue.

2 Pet. i. 3.

SUPERIOR VALUE

OF

CHRISTIAN VIRTUE.

VIRTUE has, and ever retains, a certain value, be it as defective and imperfect as it may, in whatever perfon it is exhibited, and in whatever manner it is difplayed. Truth will ever be truth, and order be always order : and he that thinks and acts confiftently with his relationfhip to God and his connection with all within his fphere, thinks and acts confiftently with truth and the order of things ; and this, in all times and places, muft be right and good. Indeed, the principles on which a man performs what is right and good,

and

and the views wherein he does so, may weaken and obscure the value of these actions, the value of virtue; but even this cannot wholly destroy it. The gold that is not purified from its drofs, does not therefore ceafe to be gold. We fhould dread, then, to incur the juft imputation of committing an infult upon virtue, were we to pronounce, with fome antient chriftian teachers, all the virtues of the heathens, or fuch as were not chriftians, to be fplendid fins. Many of their renowned atchievements may well have been fo; as, at prefent, fo many feemingly good—very good—actions of chriftians are in reality nothing lefs than good. But, we are not, on that account, to condemn them all, and declare all the really great, and noble, and public-fpirited actions they performed, to be merely the fruit of the meaneft felf-intereft, and the bafeft paffions. No man is altogether infenfible to truth, or totally incapable of thinking and acting in con-

formity

formity to it; and whoever can do fo, can be alfo more or lefs virtuous, and act accordingly. The ftronger and more prevalent this fenfibility is, the more univerfal and active will virtue be. If, then, fenfibility be not exclufively the peculiar property of any nation, or of any man, fo neither can virtue be.

But it is with chriftian virtue as with a hundred other things. Mankind are prone to extol fome one thing of undoubted excellence, and then to think they cannot do better than to vilify not only what is at variance, but likewife whatever has moft refemblance and moft affinity with it, what comes the neareft to it, in fuch a manner as to allow it no value at all. So we often hear one virtue extolled at the expence of another; and fo, in particular, the chriftian virtue at the expence of the not-chriftian. But may not, then, two things be good or excellent, and yet one be bet-

ter

ter and more excellent than the other?
Let the not-chriftian virtue enjoy all the
value it has; refpect goodnefs of every
kind, and refpect goodnefs wherever you
find it; let juftice be done to every man,
whether he be a chriftian or not. Chriftian
virtue can lofe nothing thereby; fhe ever
remains what fhe is, and ever retains a
great fuperiority over every other kind of
virtue. Of this my prefent difcourfe fhall
give you complete conviction.

We have already inveftigated the value
of feveral things that have an influence on
human happinefs; the value of riches, of
honours, of fenfible and fpiritual pleafures,
of piety, of fenfibility, and virtue; we have
fhewn you that virtue far excels all the
former: we propofe to-day to endeavour
at convincing you of the fuperiority or the
excellency of the value of chriftian virtue,
when compared with all other virtue, and
thereby increafe your reverence for it.

Thefe

Thefe reflections will convince us how true that is which the apoftle Peter affirms : God hath imparted to us chriftians, by the knowledge of Jefus Chrift, or by the chriftian religion, as much of his godly power as we had need of for leading a pious and a virtuous life. That is : by the chriftian doctrine, and its divine influence upon us, the leading of a holy life is rendered much eafier to us, and we may advance farther in virtue and piety, than we could do otherwife. And this we will take upon us circumftantially to explain and demonftrate.

You know what it is we underftand by virtue in general. We mean the difpofition of our mind, the direction and adaptation of its faculties in fuch a manner as that we conftantly think, will, and act, confiftently with truth, order, and the will of God ; the univerfal, prevalent, operative inclination to every thing that is true, and right, and good, in conformity to our nature
ture

ture and connections, and the nature and relations of other things ; the conftant readinefs to do or not to do, to fuffer or to bear, to be and to have, or not to be and not to have, what God wills us to do, or not to do, to bear or fuffer, be and have, or not to be and not to have ; the truth and harmony of all the parts of our inward and outward conduct between themfelves and with the law of God. In this, undoubtedly, confifts the effence of all virtue.

Now, if it be the doctrines of chriftianity which give this direction and adaptation to our mind and its faculties ; if it be the doctrines of chriftianity that produce in us thefe predominant difpofitions to truth and order, to whatever is right and good, and in every cafe the beft ; if it be the doctrines of chriftianity which fo abfolutely fudue our inclinations to the will of God; if it be gratitude for the benefits which God hath done us by his fon Jefus, and for the

hopes

hopes to which he hath advanced us ; if it be an intimate and hearty love to God, and love to our Lord and Saviour, which excites us to fuch a difpofition, and to fuch a conduct, which produces in us fo beautiful a harmony between all our thoughts, inclinations, propenfities, and actions; if it be the precepts and example of Jefus which conduct and lead us to it; if it be his fpirit, his mind, which lives and governs in us, and are difplayed by us : then is our virtue chriftian virtue ; it fubfifts in us by chriftianity; it is nourifhed and ftrengthened in us by chriftianity; it is framed upon the doctrines and commands of chriftianity; it is nothing elfe but vital, effective, and practical chriftianity.

Now, to fuch a chriftian virtue we afcribe a fuperior value; and this it actually poffeffes, whether we confider it in regard to its fources, or its ftandard, or its motives, or its extent, or its views. In all
thefe

thefe particulars it is purer, greater, firmer, more active, more beneficial, more bleffed, than it would be without the help of chriftianity; in all thefe particulars it therefore excels every other virtue which is deftitute of this help. Not to dwell now upon the feveral comparifons neceffary for the demonftration of this, we fhall only examine what chriftian virtue more peculiarly is, and then leave you to draw your own conclufions of its excellency.

The fources, then, from whence it fprings are the pureft; the grounds on which it refts are the firmeft, and the moft adapted to the nature of man. It is the fruit of an altered and ameliorated heart; a heart, as it were, new-formed by the doctrines of chriftianity: or, if it have taken early poffeffion of it, before vice can have ftruck its roots therein, then is it the frame and condition of a fpirit impregnated with thefe doctrines, and formed upon them; then
their

their roots lie deep; take faft hold; extend themfelves through all the faculties and all the conduct of the man ; and inter-weave, infinuate, and affimilate themfelves with his whole nature. Chriftian virtue is not an accidental, tranfient effect of parti-cular thoughts and emotions, but the ef-fect and refult of the whole thinking and fenfitive fyftem. Its force and duration is not dependent on this or that particular idea, but on an intire indivifible confe-quence of the grandeft and moft exalted truths. It grounds itfelf on all that chrif-tianity tells us of God, his attributes, his providence, his conduct towards us, and particularly of his love and clemency to weak, and finful, and guilty creatures ; on all that it difcovers to us of our nature, our origin, our vocation, the general judge-ment, and the future remuneration ; on all it teaches us concerning Jefus, of his great bufinefs upon earth, of his affiftance to mankind, of his holy life and beneficial

death,

death, of his connection with us, of his dominion over us, of his love towards us, and of his spirit in us. When these doctrines present themselves to a man, as undeniable godly truths; when he feels their truth, their certainty, their importance, feels how intimately they are connected with his present and future happiness; when they stream their radiant light upon his mind, and operate in their whole force upon his heart; when he is deeply affected by the love of God and of his son Jesus; when he is filled with sincere remorse at the sight of his sins; when his gratitude is awakened, and his love inflamed; when he has learnt to use and enjoy the promised assistance from on high; when he perceives and feels that all this is granted him by the pure bounty of God, how wretched he should be, and how miserable and deplorable he should continue, without it; how happy he is rendered by it, and how much more he may and shall be so; when he feels

7

that

that he has the happiness to be a christian, called to a blessed immortality, constantly strives to render himself more capable and worthy of this happiness, to draw nigher to his God and his Saviour, and all these dispositions and feelings are predominant in him : then he obtains, as it were, a new spirit and a new heart, becomes a new creature,—is virtuous, and christianly virtuous. And who sees not how pure, how rich, how inexhaustible, this source of virtue must be in him? on what solid foundation the edifice of such a virtue rests! how differently must all these doctrines, and the blessed alteration effected by them in his whole frame, act on him! how much more life and power to goodness must they impart to him, than the bare representation, however just and true, of the fitness or unfitness of things, of their natural relationships, ends, and powers! how much more adapted are they to the nature and capacities of man, and indeed to all particular

cular

cular men, however different their proportion of comprehenfion and their fenfibility
may be!

The rule of chriftian virtue—and this is
its fecond advantage—the rule of chriftian
virtue is more fixed, more fure, more infallible, and more ufeful than any other.
God hath, indeed, infcribed all his laws
upon our hearts; but how much have prejudices, errors, the lufts, and the paffions,
obfcured this heavenly writing, with the
generality of men! with how many are
they thus rendered illegible! with how
many are they totally effaced!—God hath
indeed made us all capable of a lively fentiment, a quick and certain judgement of
what is good and bad, and right and
wrong: but how feldom is this faculty fo
unfolded and improved, how feldom is
this judgement fo exercifed and fharpened,
as to be a fafe and certain guide to us in
all events! How often, on the contrary,

is this fentiment ftifled by the multitude of
oppofite practices, cuftoms, and examples,
and this judgement perverted by the arti-
fices of felf-love! How often, therefore,
muft even the upright man, the friend of
virtue, who has no other guide than thefe,
be deficient in neceffary certainty and refolution! how often, where his path divides
into two, muft he be liable to take the
wrong!

A miftake, which the friend of chriftian
virtue far lefs frequently falls into, which
he may totally avoid, if he adheres to the
directions given him. His path is pointed
out before him: he finds in every part of
it the footfteps of his leader and precurfor,
Jefus. Here are the exprefs precepts and
commands of God, his Lawgiver, and his
Father. This is the way thou fhalt go;
thou fhalt not turn afide to the right hand
or to the left! There is the example of
Jefus, our captain and lord. As he was
difpofed,

difpofed, fo muft thou, his difciple and follower, be difpofed ; as he walked, fo muft thou alfo walk. How can I ftand hefitating there, how fall into error, how come fhort of my mark ? As a chriftian, I believe in God, and believe in Jefus ; I confidently truft myfelf to God, my heavenly Father, and to his Son, my Saviour and Lord ;—I know that God loves me ; I know that Jefus loves me ; I know that my Creator and my Redeemer would nothing more than my happinefs,—I therefore do, what God bids me do ; abftain from what he bids me avoid ; endure what he bids me to undergo ;—follow as Jefus leads, tread confidently in his footfteps, form myfelf upon his fpirit, think and act as he thought and acted : frequently afk myfelf, what would he have done, or not have done, in my circumftances and condition ?—And while I do thus, how can I—I repeat my interrogation—how can I then ftand hefitating, how go aftray, how wander from my mark ?

mark? My leader is infallible; his precepts are godly truth. My path is luminous; it shews itself distinctly from all by-paths and devious ways; it does not wind its course in gloomy labyrinths; it leads strait forward to the mark; constantly grows smoother and plainer, the nearer it brings me to it.—With what comfortable assurance, then, may I walk therein! how securely pursue my course! to what a certainty and firmness will it bring me in the practice of virtue!

The sphere of christian virtue is likewise far more wide, its activity greater than the sphere and activity of any other virtue. Christianity, and Christianity alone, teaches us to consider all things, the small as well as the great, the seemingly insignificant as well as the more important, so much in their dependance upon God; connects all so closely with his will; unites our whole present life, with all its affairs, its pleasures,

and

and its purpofes, fo intimately and indiffolubly with our future exalted ftate; calls us to look fo ftedfaftly at God and Jefus, that, with the man that is totally animated by the fpirit of chriftianity, all is virtue,— all, even his moft inconfiderable actions, are the fruits and productions of virtue. "Whether, therefore," as it is written, "he eateth or drinketh, or whatfoever he doth, he doth all to the glory of God." "Whatfoever he doth in word or deed, he doth all in the name of the Lord Jefus, giving thanks to God and the Father by him." To the chriftian nothing is proportionately indifferent, nothing unimportant: the fpirit which lives and governs in him, ennobles all he thinks and does. His meditations on God, his joyfulnefs in him, his eager defires to pleafe him, his profpects in futurity, give life, and dignity, and confequence, to every thing he meets with, and every thing he is employed in. He confiders, judges, does, enjoys, and endures all
things

things in the light of godly truth—all things as a chriftian. Every bufinefs of his calling is to him·a commiffion from God; every infurmountable difficulty he meets with in it, is a prohibition of God; every favourable circumftance, the affiftance and the bleffing of God; every pleafure, and every fuccefs, a benefaction of God; every misfortune, a chaftifement of his love; every good and every wicked man, an inftrument in his hand. His whole life, therefore, is one continued obedience, a conftant refignation to the will of heaven, and a filial reverence of the good pleafure of God. His virtue, then, comprehends and embraces all things, combines all with each other and with God; limits him to no place, to no time, to no ftation; and the fphere of his activity is as large as the fphere of his thoughts, his fenfations, his affairs, his pleafures, the combinations of his joys and his forrows!

And

And no wonder, Sirs, that the virtue of the chriftian comprehends fo much, and operates fo far. The incitements, the motives he has thereto as a chriftian, are far more various and forcible than any others. They affect his heart while they employ his mind. They fubdue all his defires, and captivate his fenfibility, till they have convinced his reafon. Chriftianity is ordained for all mankind, and ftill more for the man of fenfibility than for the man of cold abftracted reflection. What the philofophers call truth, order, and the fitnefs of things, is here termed the command of God, our Creator and Lawgiver; the exprefs will of our fupreme Benefactor; the precept, admonition, and example of a Saviour and Redeemer, who died out of love to us; it is the only means of pleafing this indulgent God, of delighting this generous Redeemer, and of fharing in his power and glory; it is the way that leads to a bleffed immortality, to the poffeffion

of

of the moft exalted prerogatives, to the
fruition of the pureft joys in a better
world. Here all the fprings of action in
man are fet in motion, whatever ufually
incites him to the ufe of his faculties, and
renders him fteady in the exertions of
them: reverence, gratitude, love, refignation, joy, hope; defire of applaufe, thirft
after pleafure, after perfection, after happinefs. And what effects muft this produce in the human heart! And what a
mighty force muft their united powers afford for combating againft error, againft
the authority of cuftom, and the influence
of bad example!

How can I forbear to love God, the
God who loved me fo much, fo inexpref-
fibly, as to ordain Jefus to be my Saviour;
who, through him, has exalted me to the
dignity of being his fon, and called me to
fupreme felicity? And how can I love
him, this God, unlefs I keep all his com-
G 4   mandments,

mandments, and conform my whole will
to his?—How can I revere Jefus, the fon
of his love, who humbled himfelf fo far
for mankind, did and fuffered for them fo
much, imparted to them fo much illumi-
nation, fo much comfort, freedom, hope,
and happinefs? how admire him who died
upon the crofs, and thereby delivered me
from the dread of death? how connect myfelf moft intimately with him? how honour
him as my Lord and King, unlefs I give
myfelf wholly to him, unlefs I be ready to
do and to fuffer, to hazard and to facrifice
every thing for him who furrendered and
facrificed fo much for me, who even laid
down his life for my fake?———How can I
expect his laft advent to judgement with
fatisfaction to myfelf, unlefs I conftantly
am preparing myfelf for it by a holy conduct and godly means? how tranfport myfelf in fpirit into the abode of the bleffed,
which he hath prepared and opened for
me, and here not think and live as that
                                    higher

higher ſtate requires ?—And if I love God, if I love Jeſus ; if I have an inſight into futurity ; if I feel how much, how infinitely much, I owe to God and to his ſon Jeſus ; how bleſſed I am already in the enjoyment of theſe benefits, and how much more bleſſed I ſhall hereafter be ; what duty will then be too hard for me ; what ſacrifice, that God ſhall require of me, too coſtly ; what ſin will not be hateful to me; what opportunity for doing good, and for becoming uſeful to my brethren, like Jeſus, will not be right welcome to me ? Certainly he that thinketh thus—and thus muſt the chriſtian think, who is a chriſtian in deed and in truth—cannot be wanting in incitements, in deſire, in ability to do good; hath more and ſtronger motives to be virtuous, and conſtantly to improve in virtue, than any other man who has not the happineſs to be a chriſtian.

And

And how much more noble and grand are, laftly, the views of chriftian virtue! how much fuperior and more excellent the mark at which it aims! All virtue has in view the promoting of what is true, and beautiful, and good; all virtue aims at order, at perfection, at happinefs; but not as chriftian virtue does. The greater and jufter the knowledge is which the chriftian has of God, of Jefus, of the chief end of man, and of futurity, fo much the nobler muft be his fentiments, fo much more comprehenfive his views, fo much more exalted the purpofe he purfues.—The whole human race is but one large family to him, and that the family of God, his heavenly Father; a family which he embraces with his benevolence, and vifits with his love; and his affectionate activity is circumfcribed by no falfe patriotifm, is weakened by no prejudices of rank or nation. Jefus is to him, Jefus that is highly exalted over all, is to him the Lord and King of men; truth and virtue, freedom and

and happinefs, are the privileges and diftinctions of his kingdom ; and every word,
every deed, every facrifice, every fuffering
whereby the chriftian can bring one man
from error to truth, from vice to virtue,
from bondage into freedom, whereby he
can amend, confole, or rejoice him, is to
him an enlargement and confirmation of
the glorious kingdom of Jefus, an actual
participation in his great work upon earth.—
To him this life is the porch or veftibule
of the future, the preparation to it : and
all that he does and operates here, and occafions others to do and effect; all the
harm that he here prevents ; all the good
he here performs ; all the feed he fows in
this earthly foil ; all the germs he brings
to fruit ; are to him caufes that infinitely
extend in effects. This is the feed-time, of
which he expects hereafter to reap a harveft of a thoufand-fold. What profpects!
What extenfive, what comprehenfive views
does the virtue of the chriftian open before

fore him! He promotes the gracious purpofes of God with regard to man, and
labours in fellowfhip with him, his heavenly Father, for the benefit of his children; efpoufes the caufe of truth, of integrity, of freedom, the caufe of God, according to the utmoft of his power; pro-
fecutes the work that Jefus began on earth,
and enlarges the limits of his kingdom;
affifts mankind, his brethren, in their progrefs towards heaven; and is ufeful to
them, not only here, not only long after his
death, but even to eternity. How much
muft fuch profpects as thefe ennoble all
his virtuous endeavours and actions! Can
the imagination frame any loftier, any
more extenfive purpofes than thefe?

And will they ever allow him to be
weary or difheartened in his endeavours to
amend himfelf and others? Will they ever
allow him to fet bounds to his wifdom, his
goodnefs, and his general utility; ever to
think

think that he has done too much, or even
enough? No; his aim is perfection,
chriftian perfection, a conftant endeavour
at a nearer refemblance to Jefus, a conftantly nearer approximation to God.
Nothing fhort of this can fatisfy him.
The ftandard by which he meafures the
value or the magnitude of his virtue, is
not the judgement of the world, but the
judgement of heaven; not what he is and
does, but what he can do, and what he
may be. Even when he has laboured long
at his improvement, has already made great
advances, already done much, brought
much about, and fuffered much, he ftill
exclaims, with the apoftle, " Not that I
" have already attained or am already per-
" fect." No; I forget thofe things that
are behind; I fcarcely make account of
what I have already done and performed,
while fo much remains for me to do; I
prefs forward, after the higher degrees of
perfection I have not yet attained, after the

prize

prize of the mark of righteoufnefs and integrity I have then to expect when I fur-
mount all things, and perfevere unto the
end.

Yes, this is thy generous difpofition,
this thy peculiar and thy folemn language,
thou beft and fureft guide of man, O
chriftian virtue!—Bleffed be thy arrival
upon earth! and bleffed the Lord who
brought thee amongft men, and laid the
foundations of thy empire in their hearts!
Gentle is thy fway, and obedience to thee
is liberty and peace. Thou giveft ftrength
to the weary, and power to the impotent.
Thou lifteft up the poor out of the mire;
thou exalteft the humble and meek.
Thou bleffeft him with the fentiment of
his prefent and future dignity. Thou art
divine wifdom to the unlearned as well as
to the learned. Thou giveft refolution to
the irrefolute; infpireft the dead with life,
and the timid with the courage of heroes.
The

The miferable is indebted to thee for his fweeteft comfort, the defpifed good man for the inward repofe of his fpirit, the victim of perfecution for the confcioufnefs of his righteoufnefs and fidelity, the fufferer for his filent perfevering courage, and the dying man for his joyful hopes. Thou haft performed numberlefs noble deeds, and daily performeft numberlefs more, which never come to the knowledge of any mortal, which are fullied by no vain renown, which he only fees who fees in fecret, and which under his infpection never ceafe to fpread happinefs and joy through all the extent of his kingdom. O that thy predominance were univerfal! that every chriftian were animated by thy warmth! and that every chriftian, who hath not yet done it, might take thee for his model!

Yes, Sirs, this may the chriftian, and this muft he be! The light of the world, the

the falt of the earth, the inftructor, the
pattern, the improver, the helper, the
faviour of the reft of mankind; a far more
wife, more virtuous, and more ufeful citi-
zen, a far greater benefactor to his brethren,
than the wifeft, the beft of men, who is
not a chriftian! This is his calling, this
his election; and this muft be the aim of
his endeavours!

And it promifes him, both in this and
in the future world, far greater happinefs
than to any other wife and virtuous man.
Every degree of virtue renders us propor-
tionably fit for happinefs; wherefore let
us, no more than God, exclude any good
man from all felicity. But chriftian virtue
is the way that leads to the pureft and the
fublimeft blifs.—Walk then therein, O thou
that haft the happinefs to be called a
chriftian. This thou muft do, if thou
wouldft efcape eternal ruin, or be placed in
a ftate not altogether wretched. Wouldft
thou

thou be a chriftian indeed, and turn the
privileges of chriftianity to thy real advantage, then muft thou think more generoufly, and ftrive at greater attainments, at
fuperiority over all thy brethren who are
not chriftians; afpire after a higher felicity,
that hereafter thou mayft be, ftill more
than here, the leader, the teacher, the
benefactor, the helper, of thy lefs perfect
and lefs happy brethren; that thou mayft
be conftantly approaching nearer to God,
acquiring a greater refemblance to Jefus,
and mayft have evermore communion and
fellowfhip with the Father and with his Son.
What a profpect! O let it be ever prefent
to our minds, to our conftant improvement
in all chriftian virtue, conftantly bringing
us nearer to perfection!

THE
V A L U E
OF

RELIGION IN GENERAL.

This is life eternal, that they might know thee
the only true God, and Jesus Chrift, whom
thou haft fent.   John xvii. 3.

H 2

THE

VALUE

OF

RELIGION IN GENERAL.

RELIGION, Sirs,—I ſpeak of true religion, founded on reaſon and revelation,—religion is very differently judged of by different perſons. One man deems it of little or no value, and another eſteems it beyond all price. The former holds it to be a hard and fruitleſs employment of the mind; while the other takes it for the moſt important, the moſt bleſſed occupation of the heart and life. To the former it is a heavy and oppreſſive yoke, which he endeavours by all means to ſhake off, a grievous reſtraint upon his freedom and

H 3 inclina-

inclinations, a cruel difturber of his joys, which he removes from himfelf as far as he can ; to the latter it is the gentleft ruler, the kindeft and moft generous friend and comforter, the moft fertile fource of fatiffaction and joy. The firft, therefore, meddles but feldom with it, confines it to certain times and places, and finds neither comfort nor benefit in it; the fecond never lofes it out of his fight, makes it his conftant companion and guide along the path of life, and is continually receiving peace, and pleafure, and affiftance from it.

And we, Sirs, to which of thefe two claffes of perfons do we belong ? What is religion to us ? How much value has it in our eftimation ? Of what importance is it to our heart ? What influence has it on our lives ? At leaft we cannot be quite indifferent about it ; otherwife we fhould not frequent the affemblies of fuch as worfhip God and Chrift ; fhould there difcover

neither

neither attention nor fentiment; and not do many things which we now do, nor negleƈt many others which we now negleƈt. But whether we acknowledge its whole worth; whether we revere it as the moſt precious gift of heaven; whether we prize it as highly as it deſerves; whether it be as dear, as advantageous, and as confortable to us, as it may and ought; are queſtions which I can only anſwer for myſelf, and not for others. Religion is to me the moſt important, moſt indiſpenſable, and moſt exalted matter of which I can frame an idea, the greateſt benefit for which I ſtand indebted to heaven. It leads me more ſafely than any other light. It procures me more advantage and comfort, makes me more chearful and happy, than any other knowledge or ſcience, privilege or poſſeſſion, is able to do. Nor can I once forget its value, or in the ſmalleſt degree depart from its direƈtions to virtue and happineſs,

with-

without fuffering manifold detriment and prejudice.

Whoever thoroughly examines it, and fincerely follows its injunctions, muft find it prove what I have pronounced it to be. There are two matters, whereon, to this end, we muft reflect.

The firft is, how our religion muft be framed, and how we are to be difpofed towards it, if we would experience the great advantages of it.

The next, whence it receives its value, or wherein it confifts.

Religion that is founded on error, and degenerated into gloomy fuperftition; religion which confifts in empty celebrations and ceremonies, or in the fterile belief of incomprehenfible things; religion which only employs the mind of a man, as a science,

ſcience, as a theory of certain phænomena
in the phyſical and moral world, but leaves
his heart unamended and unmoved; religion which is not altogether moral, not
immediately directed to the improvement
of mankind, or which is even favourable
to ſin and vice; ſuch a religion has indeed
no value; and far be it from me to praiſe
it for its excellency, or to ſay a word in its
behalf. No, that religion alone which is
built upon truth; which teaches us our
duty to God, and to think and live in conformity to it; which provides for our manifold wants; which renders us wiſer and
better, and which is adapted and deſigned
in all its parts to promote our perfection
and happineſs; this alone hath any real
worth, this alone hath any title to our pro-
foundeſt veneration and moſt cordial love.
And of this kind is whatever we learn, by
reflecting on the world, and rational meditation on God and the proper end of man:
of this kind is that, in particular, which
God

God.hath revealed to us of himself and his will, by his fon Jefus. This is life eternal, to know thee, the only true God, and Jefus Chrift, whom thou haft fent.

But that this true, particularly that the chriftian religion, which we revere as the moft formal and moft perfect means of revelation, may be valuable and excellent to us, before all things, we muft underftand it. We muft acquire juft and clear conceptions of its contents, of its defigns, of its doctrines, precepts, and promifes. Neither the name, nor the confeffion, nor a blind reverence of religion, will make us wifer, better, and happier. It does not operate upon us like a magical charm, without our knowledge or concurrence, but only in proportion as we underftand it, reflect upon it, and actually ufe it. Attend therefore, O man, attend in this defign to the voice of God in nature, to the voice of thy Creator and Father, who fpeaks to thee

in

in all his works; and confine thyfelf to the
writings of the evangelifts and apoftles,
who deliver to thee the doctrine of Jefus in
its primitive fimplicity and purity. If
thou hearkeneft with attention to that
voice, and draweft from thefe copious
fources of truth, then will religion, devoid
of all human interpolations and inventions,
appear to thee with the moft venerable
afpect, in her majeftic unvarnifhed beauty,
as a daughter of heaven, whom the Father
hath fent to mankind for their confolation
upon earth.

Would we, farther, have religion to be
really and excellently valuable to us, then
muft we be affured of its truth, and of its
divine defcent. We muft believe it, and
believe it on principle, with fatisfying
certainty. So long as I am doubtful in
this refpect; fo long as I take its doctrines
for only probable conjectures, its precepts
for well-meant ufeful rules of life, its pro-

2   mifes

mifes for defireable events; fo long may I eafily efteem and admire it to a certain degree, and it may have a certain influence on my fentiments and my conduct : but I fhall not experience its whole force to my amendment and my comfort; I fhall not become fo good, and fo happy, as I may and fhall when I accept its doctrines for truths of demonftration, its precepts as the laws of my Supreme Sovereign and Judge, and its promifes as infallible affurances of the true and unchangeable God. This belief only, then, makes religion intrinfically facred and important to me; this belief only, then, gives her the appearance and the power fhe neceffarily ought to have, when I take her for the governefs of my heart, and the conductrefs of my life.

Yet even this is not enough. Would we have her to be to us, and to perform for us, what fhe is ordained to be and to perform, then muft we not only know and

believe

believe her, but fuffer ourfelves to be accompanied and guided by her. We muft follow her directions to virtue and happinefs, fubmit to her inftructions, be animated by her fpirit, and frame our whole behaviour on her precepts. She requires obedient and teachable difciples : fhe inftructs, fhe improves, fhe comforts us, but not againft our will, or without our concurrence. She offers the moft falutary aliment to our curious and inquifitive fpirit; but we muft take and enjoy this aliment, if we would have it to ftrengthen and refrefh us. She will lead us by the hand on the way of virtue and happinefs; but we muft actually walk that way, and purfue it with a firm and ftedfaft ftep, if we would have her for our companion, and be comforted by her affiftance. She promifes us light, and help, and fupport ; but we muft accept and ufe this light, this help, and this fupport, if we would profit by her offers. Wouldft thou, then, learn how properly

perly to eftimate the value of religion, furrender thyfelf wholly to her direction, fubmit thyfelf to her guidance in all times, in
all places, under all events. Think conftantly as fhe teaches thee to think; do
conftantly that which fhe calls thee to do;
abide ftedfaftly by that which fhe tells thee
and promifes thee on the part of God.
Separate not from her in thy ordinary, thy
daily courfe. Confine her not to the times
and places deftined to worfhip and devotion : call her not to thee barely to foothe
thee in thy forrows, and to comfort thee
in thy diftrefs. She defpifes the friends
and admirers, who only fly to her in mif-
fortunes, in idle or melancholy hours, but
drop all acquaintance with her when fuccefs fmiles upon them. No; fhe muft be
thy counfellor in all thy undertakings and
affairs, thy companion in folitude and in
fociety, thy clofe and familiar friend in
profperity and in adverfity, in life and in
death ! Then wilt thou confefs her entire

worth, and receive more fubftantial benefit from her, than from any thing whatever
that mankind can poffefs.

And how great, how great indeed, is the
value of religion to him who thus underftands her, thus trufts in her, thus follows
her fuggeftions in all his conduct, and fo
intimately attaches himfelf to her by fenfibility and reflection! O could I reprefent to you her value, as I feel it myfelf,
and render her as important to your under-
ftandings and your hearts, as fhe is to me!
It is religion that makes me wife; fhe
makes me good; fhe makes me contented
and chearful; fhe teaches me how to ufe
and enjoy the prefent; fhe opens to me the
lovelieft profpects in futurity; there promifes me a higher, an eternal felicity, and
at the fame time renders me actually capable of it. Knowledge of truth, inclination and power to do good, a tranquil and
contented heart, moderation in profperity,

com-

comfort and fortitude in adverfity, hope and affurance in life and death: thefe are thy gifts, O Religion! and how precious, how indifpenfable to my happinefs!

Religion makes me wife; fhe leads me to the knowledge of truth, the moft important, the moft indifpenfable, the moft facred truth! Without her, I fhould wander in darknefs, roam about a labyrinth of doubt, in ignorance of my origin, miftaking my object; all that furrounds me, all that happens to me and to others, would be myftery, indiffoluble myftery, to me; effects without caufes, means without end, faculties without proper directions, numberlefs feries and confequences of things without an intelligible connection, beauty, and order, produced from chance; virtue and vice, life and death, at inceffant variance; moral creatures without confiftency; an immenfe world without a fovereign and ruler; this would be the ap-

pearance

pearance of vifible things to me, and how muft fuch a view perplex my fpirit! In what a dreadful abyfs of doubt and defpondency muft it fink me! Loft among the innumerable multitude of things which belong to this univerfe, alone and abandoned amidft all the living creatures that furround me, nothing whereon to fix; nothing wherein to truft; nothing that could lead me with fafety in my thoughts and purfuits; nothing that I could confider as the fixt object of my wifhes, my defires, and my endeavours; nothing that could unite me with other beings and things! Like a child, which cruelty or accident had abandoned to itfelf foon after its birth, I fhould not know whom I had to thank for my being and my life, from whom I might expect the fupport of it, who would take care of me, to whom I might look up for protection and help, and paternal love!

VOL. II.   I   But

But thou, O divine Religion! thou freeſt me from this diſtreſſing perplexity; thou leadeſt me forth from this labyrinth of doubt, and guideſt me in the way of truth and aſſurance. Thou introduceſt me to God, and to the knowledge of the regard in which I ſtand towards him. Thou giveſt an Author, a Preſerver, a Ruler, and a Father, to me and to the whole world; and there-by diffuſeſt a light over all things, uniteſt all together, communicateſt life and order, importance and dignity to all. I now per-ceive that I am no longer loſt and forgotten in the immenſity of ſpace; am no longer the pitiable ſport of chance or fate; no longer an inſignificant, feeble, wretched creature, dependant on nothing, ignorant of its origin and end; wandering, without protector or guide, through the wilderneſs of life, this day or the next to become a prey to death. Under thy directions I have diſcovered God, have found a Father, the wiſeſt, the beſt of Fathers, who knows and

loves

loves me; and I am his creature, his child, am formed after his likenefs, am capable of his correfpondence, am and live and fubfift in him and by him; know to what purpofe he hath fafhioned and ordained me; dwell under his infpection and care; know his tender difpofitions towards me, and nothing can deftroy the bleffed connection which binds me with him unalterably and for ever.

And how differently now does every object appear to me! What a totally different, what a brighter and more chearful afpect does the world now wear to me, and how its greatnefs and beauty exalts and rejoices my fpirit! Now I perceive and revere a firft, eternal, and all-perfect Caufe of every thing which is, and was, and will be; a God from whom all things proceed, by whom they are, and to whom they belong; a God extolled and praifed by every particle of matter, every plant, every

beaft,

beaft, every man, every fpirit, the heavens
and the earth, as Almighty and All-wife,
as the Being who is love itfelf.   I now behold, on all fides, as far as my eye can furvey, or my penetration reach, the pureft
beauty and the moft harmonious order; all
around me the wifeft and beft defigns, and
the fitteft means for their completion; on
all fides life, and joy, and happinefs, here
in culture and in bud, there in bloom and
in maturity.   Now all things depend in
the clofeft and moft intimate union on each
other, the fmall and the great, the vifible
and the invifible, the grain of fand on the
fhore of the ocean, and the all-chearing
fource of light; all is the work of one
fingle and all-perfect Spirit; ai form but
one whole; one intire whole, in which the
natural and the moral, the good and the
bad, the prefent and the future, are infe-
parably bound and interwoven together;
in which nothing is unneceffary, nothing
fuperfluous, nothing unintended, nothing

I   purely

purely bad and hurtful; an intire whole, which is supported and maintained by its infinite Author himself, which he disposes and guides, and wherein all tends to the greatest possible perfection and happiness. And to know this, to be assured of these most sublime, most fruitful, and most comfortable truths; to have them for the directing clue to our reflections and researches, for the rule of our behaviour, for the ground of our desires and hopes, is this not wisdom? Is it not greater, and sublimer wisdom, than all else that usually bears the name? And must not the religion which leads us to this wisdom, be of inestimable value to us? Must it not be the most precious gift of heaven?

As religion makes me wise, it also renders me good; and this is a second demonstration of its superior worth and excellency. Religion is the band of love, the intimate tie of union between the Crea-

tor

tor and his creatures, and between all
thinking, feeling, and rational creatures
with each other, the principle of the clofeſt
connection of the natural with the moral
world, and the prefent with the future.
And this love, this connection, this union,
produces in every human heart it animates
new fpiritual life, freſh inclination and
power to all goodnefs; more fpiritual vigour, more defire and ability to duty and
to virtue, than any other confideration,
any other relation of things can do.   And
fûrely, when I know and venerate a God,
who is my Creator, my Preferver, my Benefactor, my Father, my Sovereign, and my
Judge, and who hath given me laws, and
hath annexed the moſt glorious rewards to
the obfervance of them, and the fevereſt
punifhments to the violation of them; thefe
laws muſt be of the utmoſt importance to
me! How facred, how inviolable, muſt
they be! And when I behold this God
every where in his works; hear his in-
ſtructing,

structing, his inciting and his warning voice,
on every side I turn; feel myself encom-
passed by him and the effects of his wisdom; revere him, wherever I am, in the
thickest veil of darkness no less than in the
brightest day, as the witness of my thoughts
and actions: how shall I dare to think or
to do any thing that militates with his will,
or neglect any thing that he has enjoined?
How can I be deficient in courage and ability, in his presence and under his inspec-
tion, to do readily and heartily that which
is right and good, and best for the occa-
sion? And if I love this God, this Father,
as religion teaches me, with filial affection,
think on him, and raise myself to him with
inward pleasure, rejoice in his existence, in
his presence, in his bounty, in his dispositions towards me, and his communion with
me: how easy and agreeable it must be to
me to keep his commandments, to concur
with his designs, and to labour, as it were,
in fellowship with him for advancing the

I 4   univer-

univerfal perfection and felicity of his kingdom!

But, as religion connects the creatures with the Creator, fo likewife does it connect the creatures with each other; fo does it unite me alfo with all my fellow-mortals; it teaches me that they are all children of my heavenly Father, that we all compofe but one large family, whofe father is God, and whofe firft-born brother is his fon Jefus. And, if I believe this, if I have an inward fentiment of this, I then live among my own brothers and fifters, who have the fame origin and the fame deftination with myfelf: and, then, how muft the fight of every man, how muft the difpofitions, the capacities, the abilities of every man, the pleafures, the profperity, the merits of every man, delight me! And, if I am animated with that brotherly love towards them which religion alone can infpire, how impoffible will it be for me to deprive them

of

of their property and goods, or to difunite
or injure them by any means whatever!
How far from my heart will all pride and
envy be, all hatred and indifference! How
compaffionate fhall I be towards them,
merciful as my Father in heaven is merciful, and beneficent as he is beneficent!
And what duty towards my neighbour fhall
I then neglect? Which of them fhall I
difcharge without fidelity and pleafure?

And, if I do but feel the whole force
of the love of God and of Chrift towards
man, which the chriftian doctrine repre-
fents to us in fo affecting a manner; if I
have an inward fentiment of what great
things God hath done for me, how much
his fon Jefus hath facrificed and fuffered
for me; if I take the difpofition and life of
this my Deliverer for the rule of my conduct; if I look up to him as my Fore-
runner and Chief, and firmly confide in his
promifes; if I ferioufly confider the connection

nection of the prefent with the future, regard one as the preliminary to the other,
one as the time of fowing and the other of
reaping ; what incitement, what ability to
every thing that is right and good, that is
great and generous, muſt not all this afford !   No ; if religion does not make me
better, if it does not make me endeavour
to become a good and virtuous man, I
muſt then be incapable of amendment,
muſt be deeply funk beneath the dignity of
man, muſt have a completely infenſible and
thoroughly corrupted heart.   And what a
value muſt this likewife give to religion in
our eſteem, if we do but properly underſtand the worth of moral goodnefs and
virtue !

He that is wife and good, may alfo be
contented and chearful ; and the religion
that procures us thofe advantages, procures
us likewife thefe.   Far from infpiring her
true profeſſors with flaviſh fear and gloomy
                                    terrors,

terrors, fhe fills them with confidence and
courage. Far from being a difturber of
joy, fhe opens to us the richeft fources of
it, and invites us to them. Yes, if I follow her precepts, and believe in her promifes : then tranquillity and joy take poffeffion of my breaft ; then am I affured of
the grace of God, the forgivenefs of my
fins, the good pleafure of my Creator and
Lord ; then my heart no more torments
and condemns me ; then I enjoy the blefled-
nefs of a good confcience. Yes, if I allow
myfelf to be guided and conducted by her,
and confider all things in the light which
fhe diffufes over them ; then am I fatisfied
with all things ; fatisfied with God, whom
I know and revere as the wifeft and moft
tender Father, and from whom I expect
only good, and conftantly the beft ; fatif-
fied with all his arrangements and difpofitions in the natural and the moral world ;
fatisfied with the place and the circumftances wherein he hath fet me, with the

por-

portion of abilities and goods he hath granted me, with the term he hath allotted me, as I know that all this is adapted to my being, and defigned for my happinefs; fatisfied with myfelf, as I am confcious of my uprightnefs and integrity, as I feel, as it were, that I do not wilfully tranfgrefs, and that I am approaching nearer to the mark of chriftian perfection; fatisfied with all my fellow-creatures, as I hate none, and envy none, as I love them all, rejoice with all the good, and am patient and indulgent to the frail and infirm; fatisfied with all things about me, as every thing is, and is juft fo, as the all-wife and all-gracious God would have it to be!

Nay, when I allow myfelf to be guided by the light of Religion, and to be animated by her fpirit, I find fources of joy opening to me on all fides, as pure as they are inexhauftible; then I poffefs more real joy than the greateft darling of fortune can have, whq

who knows not this Giver of joy; then I
rejoice in God, my Benefactor and Father;
I rejoice in his fon Jefus, my Redeemer and
Lord; I rejoice in my capacities and
powers, in my high vocation; I rejoice in
all the beautiful and good that is and happens in the world; I rejoice in all mankind
as my brethren, as the children of my heavenly Father, as the partakers of my future felicity; I rejoice in every animate
and inanimate creature, as it is the creature
of my God; I rejoice in vifible and invifible things, the prefent and the future;
and am joyful that I am immortal, and
may affuredly expect an everlafting life, a
never-ending felicity. And for this chearful confidence, this fatisfaction, thefe manifold joys, I am indebted to Religion. How
can I not perceive its worth! how can I
miftake its excellency?

Yes, this it is, this divine Religion,
which conducts, ftrengthens, comforts, and
exhi-

exhilarates me, in all the viciffitudes of my circumftances, in whatever I do, and in whatever befalls me, in profperity and in adverfity, in life and in death. She gives quite another appearance to all things; fweetens every pleafure to me, and augments every good; mitigates every hardfhip, and alleviates every forrow; fupplies me with inftruction, with fupport, with confolation and affiftance. If I enjoy fatisfaction and pleafure, fhe exalts the enjoyment by infpiring me with the fentiment that it is God who giveth me this fatisfaction, who procureth me this pleafure. Have I various and important duties to fulfill, toilfome affairs to manage, fhe fo alleviates and ennobles them, by reprefenting them to me as commiffions from God, by affuring me that I am labouring in his fervice, that I difcharge my truft under his infpection, and with his concurrence. Does an opportunity occur to me for doing good, of being ufeful, and of pro-

promoting human happinefs, fhe gives me to feel the whole weight of the honour of being an inftrument in the hand of God, whereby he promotes his defigns, and diffeminates life and bleffing amongft the human race. Do I meet with difficulties on my way, do I fall into penury and danger, fhe bids me lift my eyes and my heart towards heaven, and implore and expect fuccour from him who doth what he will both in heaven and on the earth, and never willeth any thing but what is right and good. Am I oppreffed by any burden of life, fhe then bids me depend upon the fupport of him who laid this load upon me, and to be affured that he will not impofe on me more than I am able to bear. Does any misfortune overtake me, I then adore in filent reverence, as inftructed by Religion, the hand of him who inflicts it upon me, who inflicts it upon me for wife and good purpofes, and without whofe permiffion no harm can happen unto me.

3   Do

Do fufferings fall to my lot, which I have not deferved, I take them as the difpenfations of my God and Father, with filial fubmiffion; revere them as the means of nurture and exercife, by which he would lead me to higher perfection; and I know that, fooner or later, all will turn to my good. Am I alarmed and perplexed at any extraordinary or terrifying events that happen in the world, and among mankind, then, full of faith, I look up to him who governs all things, directing them by the laws of fovereign wifdom, and tranquillize my fpirit by the confideration that he will certainly, at length, bring to pafs fome good thereby. Do my honeft undertakings, my good and beneficent endeavours, fail of fuccefs, I then make an offering of my will to the far wifer and far better will of my God and Father; fatisfy myfelf with the confcioufnefs of having acted uprightly and well-pleafing to him; and therefore reckon not my pains and
labour

labour as loſt, as I know that in his kingdom, and under his adminiſtration, nothing
good can poſſibly be loſt. Do the infirmities of age oppreſs me, diminiſh my faculties, and bow down my body to the earth,
I commit myſelf to that God, who, in my
infancy, in my childhood, in my youth,
and in my manhood, has never forſaken
me, who has been conſtantly my ſupport
and my father, and will be ſo for ever.
Does death draw nigh me, does he bid me
ſet my houſe in order, and prepare to quit
all viſible and earthly things, I then hear
the voice of my heavenly Father calling
me to himſelf, calling me from the preſent
into another and a higher life, calling me
home from my pilgrimage. Conducted
and ſupported by religion, I follow this
call with joy, enter with confidence the
gloomy path of death, paſs through it un-
diſmayed, and am certain that it will terminate in the pureſt light, in unending
felicity to me.

VOL. II.   K   Thus

Thus am I taught, thus led, thus charmed, thus fupported and ftrengthened, thus comforted by religion, in profperity and adverfity, in life and in death ! Thus does fhe preferve her value in all times, in all places, in all circumftances, in regard to all my affairs, all my intentions and purfuits, unchangeably continuing what fhe is; conftantly the fafeft teacher, the moft faithful guide, and the beft comforter of man ! Yes, O divine Religion, that art thou, that wilt thou ever be to me, what thou haft hitherto been ! ever my trueft friend, my infeparable guide along the path of life, the partaker of all my joys and forrows, my confolation in death, and my conductor to the manfions of heaven ! Yes, O God ! to know thee, the only true God, the all-wife, the all-bountiful, the Father of men, to know thee, and him whom thou haft fent, our Saviour Jefus, this is life eternal, the fupreme, everlafting blifs !

ESTI-

ESTIMATE XV.

THE

VALUE

OF THE

CHRISTIAN RELIGION,

IN PARTICULAR.

I am come that they might have life, and that
they might have it more abundantly.
John x. 10.

K 2

THE

VALUE

OF THE

CHRISTIAN RELIGION,

IN PARTICULAR.

THE arrival of a Perfon who promifes life, and more abundant life, that is, complete felicity, to them to whom he comes, and is able to fulfill his promife, muft be moft defireable to fuch as have vehement defires after happinefs, and at the fame time are oppreffed with the inward fentiment of their want of it! And who of us, Sirs, can miftake this wifhed-for Perfon, who the happy Man that brought thefe joyful tidings? How eager are all men after happinefs! and how little true

feli-

felicity, how much actual misery, was there among mortals when Jesus made his appearance in the world, and offered them their deliverance from misery, and the possession of that happiness they had so long sought for in vain! and how great a right he had to make them this offer! Knew he not all the sources of their happiness. Opened he not all of them to the human race? Where is there one that ever drew from those sources, and yet found his expectations deceived? And how many thousands, and thousands again, have actually drawn therefrom, and found their thirst after happiness assuaged!

To us also these sources stand open; and we are invited to them by the Saviour who came into the world, to impart life, and abundance of it. Let us, then, approach these sources, study to know more of these blessings, compare them with our wants and defects; and then examine whether we

may

may not be happy likewife, or whether our happinefs may not be augmented and improved.

What are, then, the principal wants of man?

And how can and will Jefus fupply them, and thereby render him happy?

To anfwer thefe queftions will be the fubject and fcope of my prefent difcourfe.

Light for the underftanding; reft for the heart; courage and ability to do good; comfort in diftreffes; hope for the future: thefe are the principal wants of man. Whoever removes thefe, delivers him from the burden of his mifery, opens to him the richeft fources of felicity, and makes him truly happy. And this the Saviour of men, who came into the world, both can and will perform. He can and will, in all thefe

K 4   refpects,

respects, give them life, and greater abundance of it.

Light for the understanding, is the first and most urgent want of the thinking man. To act with consciousness and consideration; to reflect upon what he sees, what he hears, what he feels, and what befalls him; to inquire into the causes and scope of things; to look back upon the past, to expatiate in the future, and to compare them both with the present; is the natural employment, the most essential privilege of man; it is this which renders him a man. To scrutinize after truth, and to embrace the truth, is the life and the nutriment of his spirit. But how long can he employ himself in any reflection, without entangling himself in a labyrinth, whose outlet he can never find! How far can he proceed in the investigation and the knowledge of truth, without starting at some precipice, which fills him with terror, and makes him recoil!

recoil! How foon will he be deceived by error and the prolufions of fancy, or oppreffed by ignorance or doubt, if he have no faithful conductor through the intricacies of human thought!

What am I, and what is all that furrounds me? Whence am I, and whence have all thefe arifen? To what end am I, to what end are all thefe ordained? Does intelligence prefide, or chance, wifdom, or blind neceffity, in the concatenation of things, in the occurrences of the world, in the fortunes of men? Are wifdom, virtue, and happinefs, real attainable things, or only empty names? Which is the way that leads to the knowledge of truth, to the poffeffion of virtue, to the enjoyment of happinefs? Is there a God? Is there a Providence! In what relationfhip flands this God to the world and to me? How far does this Providence extend over the world and me? What have I, in thefe refpects,

to

to hope for or to fear?—What queſtions.! How difficult to be anſwered by the man that is left to himſelf! What error is too abſurd for him to plunge into in reſearches like theſe! and yet how important is their ſolution! How every thing muſt torment a reflecting mind, that cannot account for it in any rational manner! Yes, here a man feels the want of ſome certain guide, ſome ſuperior light. Here he longs for this director, for this light, as a pilgrim, overtaken by the night in ſome lone and trackleſs wild, longs for the genial effulgence of the morning ſun, or to meet with ſome traveller acquainted with the way.

Chriſt, this bright effulgence of the glorious day, hath appeared to our relief! God hath ſent to us this faithful guide! He calls to us, in our forlorn eſtate: I am the Way, the Truth, and the Life; I am the Light of the world; he that followeth me walketh not in darkneſs. No; his divine

vine doctrine has difperfed the darknefs of
error and doubt, of ignorance and fuperftition, with which the wife and the unwife,
the learned and the unlearned, were till
then furrounded. He hath brought concealed and miftaken truth to light; and
what was but little, and that little only
doubtfully known, hath he divulged to all,
and placed it beyond all doubt. He hath
brought us to the knowledge of God, the
true, the only God, and thereby given
firmnefs and affurance to the human intel-
lects. By him enlightened, we know our
origin, and the origin of all things, our
deftination, and that of all living and fenfible beings. By him inftructed, we know
that there is a God, a fupremely perfect
Spirit, an infinitely wife and bountiful
Father of the world and of mankind, and
that we are his creatures, his children;
that we and all things fubfift under his infpection and providential care; that all is
difpofed, conducted, and governed by him,

and

and all made to conduce to the beft and worthieft purpofes.—And now chance, and hazard, and blind neceffity, with all their terrors, vanifh from before our eyès. Now no intricacies bewilder us, we are no longer perplexed by any apparent diforder and contradiction in the combination of things, in the complication of human concerns. Now light, order, beauty, perfection, are difplayed in all things; for all are effects and arrangements of fupreme benignity and wifdom. The entrance to the fanctuary of truth, the moft important, moft comfortable truth, ftand open to us; the way of virtue is made plain and bright, and leads us ftraight to the manfions of blifs, where we are all invited to the enjoyment of its treafures. We have now a certain clue to guide us through the labyrinth of afflictions, by means of which we can avoid every pit and precipice, are furnifhed with all neceffary light, and proceed to meet the full beam of day.——Yes, look

to

to Jefus for the fupply of your wants, all
you who thirft after the knowledge of
truth. Imbibe his doctrine, adhere firmly
and confidently to it, ftudy it in the writings
which fome of his intimates have left us.
They cannot, they will not lead you aftray;
you will improve conftantly in wifdom, and
acquire complete fatisfaction.

Reft for the heart; reft under the fentiment of our weaknefs; reft amidft the violence and impetuofity of the paffions; reft
under the confcioufnefs of our tranfgreffions
and fins; reft, at the fight of the feeming
perplexity in the courfe of things, and of
human mifery; reft amidft the great frailty
and inconftancy of every thing fenfible and
earthly: what requifites, what cogent requifites, are thefe! Who will fupply them?
Where fhall a man feek and find this reft?
In what fchool of wifdom, in what temple
of mirth, in what filent and defert folitude, or in what brilliant abode of pleafure,

fure, in what rank, in which of the claffes
of mankind, fhall we fearch after it and
find it? Oh, how earneftly do the wife
and the ignorant, the high and low, the
rich and the poor, the hermit and the epi-
cure, ftrive after this repofe! With what
eagernefs of expectation do they now ftrike
into this path, and then into that! and, at
length, fooner or later, affected by repeated
difappointments, how they return by the
way that they went, fighing and afhamed
at their ficklenefs and folly, and joining at
laft in that difmal complaint, All, all is
vanity, and vexation of fpirit!

But why, Sirs, why do you feek reft
where it is not to be found? O come to
him, feek it of him, who hath promifed to
give you likewife in this refpect life, and
more abundance of it! him who reftores
to men the peace which they had miftaken,
and driven from their hearts and their
dwellings! Hear what he fays to every
honeft

honeft foul which feeks that reft of him he announces on the part of God, and how he fupplies every want of the heart.

O thou, who art fenfible of thy infirmities, do not endeavour to reprefs that fentiment. God, thy Sovereign and thy Father, requires nothing of thee that thou art unable to perform. He lays no burdens on thee that are too heavy for thee to bear. Only exert thy faculties, and they will grow ftronger by exercife. He who faithfully employs the powers he has, will be ever receiving greater. Thou haft the Almighty for thy fupport; and his ftrength is mighty, above all expectation, in the feeble that look up to him, and depend upon him. At prefent thou art but a child; hereafter, if thou only retaineft the fimplicity of a child, thou wilt arrive at manhood, and fhalt perform manly actions, fuch actions as I have atchieved.

Doft

Doſt thou feel deſires within thee, which none of all the things that ſurround thee are able to appeaſe or to ſatisfy? O learn, from thence, that thou art not made for this world alone; that greater capacities, and nobler faculties, lie concealed in thee than belong to the courſe of thy life on earth. Direct thy deſires to God, and to futurity; let the love of truth, of virtue, of God and man, pervade and poſſeſs thy heart. Theſe are goods and bleſſings that are worthy thy moſt ſtrenuous endeavours, which will employ all thy faculties and powers, which leave neither repugnance nor diſguſt, nor languor nor ſatiety, behind them. Wage war, then, againſt pleaſure and paſſion. The prize that awaits thee is worth the conflict. Whoever contendeth and conquereth here, in my cauſe, ſhall reign hereafter with me: he that loſeth his life, or any thing elſe, for my ſake, ſhall find it again.

Does

Does the confcioufnefs of thy paft fins and failings difturb thee, doft thou dread the difpleafure and the punifhment of the Judge of the world! then accept the glad tidings he commiffioned me to announce to finful man. Accept them, and rejoice that God, thy Sovereign and thy Judge, is alfo thy Father; that he is gracious and merciful, flow to anger, and of great goodnefs; that he forgives the repentant and returning finner, all his fins, remits his punifhment, reftores him to his once flighted favour, and will grant him grace for juftice. To affure thee thereof he fent me upon the earth. Sin is done away by obedience to my precepts; by following my injunctions, iniquity is remembered no more; reconcilement between God and man is thus procured by me. Only beware of the deceitfulnefs of fin; refcue thyfelf more and more from its fhameful dominion; preferve thy regained freedom; redouble thy zeal in goodnefs; devote thyfelf by gratitude

tude and love to thy gracious Benefactor and Patron, and be faithful unto the end: and then shall thy former tranfgreffions be remembered no more, and their ruinous confequences shall be removed for ever.

At times art thou difmayed at the fight of fo feemingly perplexed a fcene of things as the prefent ftate affords, and the diverfity of mifery that prevails among mankind? Tranquillize thy fpirit in the confideration of the parental providence and love of thy heavenly Father, whofe thoughts and ways are as far above thy thoughts and ways as the heavens are above the earth. Leave it to him how the world fhould be governed, and the ends of his creation obtained : and be affured that his defigns will not fail, and that his purpofe is nothing but felicity and perfection.   Judge not by that fpan of fpace, by that moment of time, which thou art allowed to furvey : extend thy comprehenfion, if thou canft, to

the

the whole, and let thy mind expatiate in eternity; and doubt not but all will be sooner or later unraveled, and shewn to be conformable to the laws of Supreme Wisdom and Goodnefs. He, the supremely Wife, the supremely Good, comprehendeth all things, can produce light out of darknefs, and turn every evil into a fource of joy.

Does the uncertainty and inftability of earthly things difmay thy fpirit, and deftroy thy peace? O learn, then, to efteem thofe things as what they really are; and while thou feeft that the world, with its pleafures, paffeth away, forget not that he who doth the will of God abideth for ever; forget not that thy fpirit is immortal, and that an unchangeable, undecaying, and incorruptible heritage is allotted thee in heaven. Soar above this tranfient fcene of vanity, and confider thyfelf as a denizen of the city of God, which hath firm foun-

L 2   dations,

dations, and is thy true, thy permanent country. Thus does Jesus inspire with peace and satisfaction the man who seeks them of him : thus does he supply all the wants of our heart : thus does he give us likewise in this respect life, and greater abundance of it.

Courage and ability in goodness is a third and no less urgent want of the thinking man. Unless this be supplied, how can he be contented and happy! He is sensible of powers, various active powers, within him. But how and to what shall he apply them? What shall he hope to execute with them? Can he, or will he, discomfit his weakness, conquer his dependance on sensible things, and overcome himself? Is not virtue too exalted for the reach of his faculties? Is she not probably designed for beings of a superior order to man? Is she not rather a daughter of heaven than the offspring of earth? As

many

many powers as he feels himself to poſſeſs, ſo many obſtacles and difficulties does he meet with in his endeavours to uſe them. Reſpectable and venerable are the dictates of reaſon; importunate and alluring are the requiſitions of ſenſe. For every incitement he perceives on one hand to goodneſs, he ſees a temptation and inducement on the other to evil. Who can proceed in ſo ſlippery a path with firm and vigorous ſteps! Who can live confident and ſecure amidſt enemies and dangers! Who can ſet himſelf to oppoſe the impetuoſity of a torrent!

The chriſtian can do it. In this reſpect alſo Jeſus gives him life, and a greater abundance of it. With him new ſpiritual life was imparted to mankind. Feeble, torpid, and dead, as the moral world appeared before his birth, it acquired a freſh activity, a nobler life, by his doctrine, by the moving of his ſpirit within it. The

L 3   way

way of virtue had been fo long abandoned, it was become a defert; thorns and briars choked up its unfrequented paths, or concealed them with impenetrable fhade: the traveller now walks them with fatisfaction and delight; Jefus has cleared them for his followers, made the crooked ftrait, and the rough places plain. He became a light to our feet, and a lantern to our paths.— Follow, then, O thou that afpireft after freedom and virtue, who wifheft to foar above fenfible things, and to become wife and good; follow the guidance of Jefus, follow his example, tread in his fteps, be a chriftian with all thy heart. This will infpire thee with new powers, and animate thee with new life. Thou wilt learn to feel the dignity of man, the dignity of a chriftian; and this fentiment will not allow thee to be wanting in courage and capacity for goodnefs. Thou wilt love God, and learn to love mankind; and this love will render every duty familiar and pleafant to thee.

thee. Chrift will live and govern in thee; his mind, his fpirit will direct thee, and through him thou canft do all things. His brilliant example will, be ever before thine eyes, conftantly alluring thee to imitation, and warning thee of every devious and oblique way; and while thou feeft the traces of his fteps before thee, thou wilt purfue thy courfe in confidence and fafety. The affurance of his fupport, the confcioufnefs of his approbation, the generous ambition of refembling him farther, and thereby becoming capable of greater felicity, will never allow thee to be faint or fatigued in the imitation of him. His promifes will ftrengthen thee. The victor's crown, he holds out to thee, at the end of thy courfe will fhine upon thee in all its radiance; and the moft glorious profpects he opens to thee, in futurity, will encourage thee to vanquifh every difficulty, firmly to brave the hardeft conflicts, and to perfevere unto the end. Yes, the faith of the

chrif-

chriftian overcomes the world, conquers all oppofition, is an inexhauftible fource of fpiritual life, and fpiritual force. So certainly as thou alloweft thyfelf to be thoroughly animated by the fpirit of chriftianity, and to be guided by its precepts, fo certainly wilt thou be thoroughly free, thoroughly virtuous, and become as perfect as a human creature can be.

Comfort in afflictions! who can deny this a place among the wants of mankind? Who has not often fel how great, how preffing it is? For who has not often fuffered, and earneftly looked around him for refrefhment and comfort? Without fuffering, no man hath ever yet finifhed his earthly courfe. To be frail and mortal, and to live among merely frail and mortal creatures and things, and to keep free from all fufferings, is a contradiction in terms. The very enjoyments of this life are, for the moft part, fo interwoven with fuffer-

2   ings,

ings, that they cannot be purely poffeffed.
And how infinitely diverfified are they!
Inward and outward fufferings; fufferings
of the mind; fufferings of the body; fufferings of affection; fufferings of friendfhip; and fufferings of virtue. And how
rapidly do they fucceed each other! How
often do they unite in numbers and in bitternefs! And what can alleviate the burden
of them to me? What can teach me to
bear them with fedatenefs and fortitude?
What can give me comfort and confidence
when I fuffer want; when I labour under
pain; when fo many attacks are made upon
my welfare and my pleafures; when oppreffed by cares and forrows; when in conflict with fuch obftacles and contradictions;
when I fail in my good defigns, and cannot
enjoy the fruit of my virtue; when my
friends forfake me, my powers decay, and
the infirmities of age opprefs me? Can I
expect affiftance from mankind, who are
as feeble as myfelf? Can riches, or honours,

nours, or diffipations, or a fplendid luxu-
rious life, affuage my pains and heal my
wounds ? Or can I be relieved by the fight
of fuch numbers of the unhappy, who
fuffer as much as myfelf, or even more
than I ?

No, my chriftian brother, this is what
Jefus alone can do. He, who himfelf did
fuffer fo much, was made perfect through
fufferings, and by fufferings entered into
his glory. He knows the fufferings of human nature, he hath undergone them himfelf, dignified them, and given them another
afpect. He can, he will confole thee; will
in this refpect likewife give thee life, and
abundance of it. Accept his offered comfort, and let him reftore thy foul. He
faith to thee, Even fufferings come from
God; they are the ordinances and difpenfations of thy Father in heaven; and whatever he, the All-wife, the All-bountiful
ordains, what he, thy Father, lays upon
thee,

thee, is good, and muſt and will advance
thy welfare. Heartily would he ſpare thee,
and all his children upon earth, from ſor-
rows, had he not in view to exerciſe and
improve thee, and attract thee to a ſuperior
life. Heartily would he grant thee pure
delights, and let all things go according to
thy wiſh, if thou wert already capable of
bearing ſuch ſuccefs. He corrects, he
proves, he exerciſes thee, becauſe he loves
thee, and becauſe his love embraces all
thy being, and provides for thy future welfare as well as for thy preſent. The path
of ſorrow is, indeed, a rough and gloomy
path ; but it leads to perfection and happineſs ſuch as firmly and piouſly purſue it.
Even ſufferings are benefits, when God inflicts them on his children, to teach them
obedience, fortitude, and faith. Even ſufferings, to ſuch as patiently endure, and
wiſely uſe them, will, ſooner or later, become a ſource of bleſſing. What they now
ſow in tears, they ſhall hereafter reap in
joy.

joy. The fufferings of this prefent time are not worthy to be compared with the glory that fhall hereafter be revealed in us. No; bear, endure, and fuffer without re-pining, and with filial refignation, what thy Father in heaven calls thee to bear, to endure, and to fuffer. He knows thy wants, and thy powers, and every burden he lays upon thee is adapted to them. He defigns thee for his kingdom, and knows how beft to prepare and fit thee for it. Look unto me, fays Jefus to his confeffors, look unto me, thy Precurfor and Guide. Bear and fuffer, as I have borne and fuffered; fight the conflicts which I have fought, and in which fo many of my followers have fuc-cefsfully ftriven. The end of thy way will be pure and exalted blifs, the prize of thy victory will be eminent glory and honour. And what can infpire us with comfort in forrows, if fuch promifes and fuch profpects are unable to do it?

Hope,

Hope, a fure and certain hope for the future, is another want of man, which it is uncommonly neceffary for him to fupply. The more tranfitory the prefent, the fhorter and more uncertain his duration here, the more fteadily muft he direct his eyes and his defires towards futurity, the lefs indifferent can he be concerning what he has there to hope for, or to fear : that, fooner or later, to-day or to-morrow, all outward vifible things will vanifh away to him, and be funk in the profoundeft obfcurity of night; that, fooner or later, to-day or to-morrow, his riches, his diftinctions, his honours, his power, his beauty, his health, all that he is and poffeffes as an inhabitant of this world, muft be loft to him ; that, fooner or later, to-day or to-morrow, a dark and lonely grave will inclofe his body, and diffolve it into duft ; that, fooner or later, to-day or to-morrow, he will quit this world, with all its glories and all its joys, and pafs into a different, to him an unknown

known ftate; is what he knows, and what he feels; this every pain declares, every infirmity, every ficknefs, the departure of every acquaintance and friend, every ftroke of the paffing-bell, every open grave, every tomb, every church-yard hillock, with an inceffant voice. And where is the man whom this does not affect, whom it does not plunge in deep reflection, whom it does not frequently alarm with concern and doubt!

Is then this night to laft for ever? Are all thefe beauties and fatisfactions to vanifh away from before me for ever? Am I eternally to lofe them all, and to be made amends for them by nothing? Am I, then, wholly duft? Is this vifionary life my whole exiftence? Do I totally ceafe to be, when my body ceafes to move, and the blood to flow in my veins? And, if that which thinks and acts within me furvive the diffolution of my body, what will be

my

my portion then? Into what region of all the immenfity of fpace fhall 1 be tranf-ported? Who will be there my Leader and Guide? What joys, or what forrows, what recompences, await me there? How is the prefent connected with the future? Oh, who will difpel this darknefs from before my eyes! who will folve thefe doubts! Who will give me that light and certainty, without which I cannot here be fatisfied!

This alfo, my chriftian brother, this alfo can Jefus do, and will; he who promifes thee life, and more abundance of it. Even this thy want he powerfully fupplies, the Conqueror of death and the grave, the Reftorer of life and felicity. He mani-fefted himfelf upon the earth to affure thee of this in the fulleft manner, to die upon the crofs, and to rife again from the dead. I, fays he, I am the refurrection and the life; he that believeth in me, fhall not die eternally; he fhall prefs through death

to

to a better life. No; this life is not the whole of thy being; it is only the firft, the loweft ftep of thy exiftence. No; thou art not wholly duft; thy fpirit is of divine defcent, it is immortal, will rife above the duft, and fhall not fee corruption. No; the night that furrounds thee in death, will not eternally, will not long endure; the morn will come, and a glorious day arife. No; the lofs thou fuffereft then is not irreparable, the friends thou then wilt lofe are not for ever loft; infinitely more joys and bleffings await thee in the future world, than thou couldft enjoy in the prefent. Therefore fhudder not thou at the prefence of death, tremble not thou at the grave, be not thou difmayed at the darknefs and gloom of the valley of the fhadow of death, nor at what will be the portion of thy heritage for ever. Be faithful to God, and to thy duty; think and live conftantly as befits a chriftian; and then will thy death be a paffage into a better, a fuperior life;

then

then wilt thou, with confidence, fee before
thee the refurrection of the dead; then
wilt thou enter the abode where thy Chief,
thy Lord, thy Redeemer is, and take part
in his glory; and he, who now is thy Example and Guide, will alfo be thy Leader
through the valley of death, thy Lord for
Eternity. There wilt thou reap the fruit
of every good thought and action, and a
conftantly increafing perfection and felicity
will be the reward of thy fidelity. What
hopes! what profpects! Animated by
thefe, how confidently may we meet futurity! how unconcernedly behold all that
is vifible and earthly, changing, revolving,
finking hence, and vanifhing away!

Thus are all our wants fupplied by Jefus.
Thus do we find light to our underftanding, reft for our heart, courage and ability
to goodnefs, comfort in forrow, hope in
futurity; thus life and abundance thereof
with him. Thus does he free us from

every kind of mifery, and lead us to the higheft felicity whereof we are capable. Oh let us, then, rejoice in him, and his entrance into the world, and his great bufinefs on earth; let us adhere firmly to him, and give up ourfelves intirely to his guidance and direction! Replete with affection and gratitude, let us profit by the fources of knowledge, of wifdom, and virtue, which he has opened to us. They are pure, and they are inexhauftible. He that drinketh of this water fhall not thirft for ever. He that draws from thefe fources, will draw joy and felicity, both for the prefent and the future life. Oh, let us all do fo. and thus affuage our thirft after truth and certainty, after peace of mind, perfection, and felicity!

ESTI-

ESTIMATE XVI.

THE
V A L U E
OF
CHRISTIANITY,

In regard of the

GENERAL ADVANTAGE

IT HAS

Procured to MANKIND, and ſtill procures.

Old things are paſt away; behold, all things
are become new.   2 Cor. v. 17.

THE
VALUE
OF
CHRISTIANITY,

In regard of the

GENERAL ADVANTAGE it has procured
to MANKIND, and ftill procures.

WE all of us enjoy the advantages
accruing to us from the appearance
of Jefus among men, and his great work
upon earth. Why are we ufed to cele-
brate the feftival of his birth, why pafs
this day more chearfully than all others?
Our joy is undoubtedly very proper and
becoming; it refts upon the moft folid
foundations, on events fuperlatively defireable

fireable and joyful. But is our joy likewife rational? Do we know, do we rightly
confider what a bleffed influence chriftianity has on our welfare, and in general on
the welfare of mankind? And is this the
reafon that the confideration of the birth of
Jefus, the founder of chriftianity, is fo joyful to us?—I fhall endeavour to advance
this knowledge, and promote thefe reflections in you, by my prefent difcourfe, and
thereby render more rational and lively the
joy the return of this day excites. We are
naturally furnifhed with an occafion hereto
by the words of our text. Old things are
paft away, fays the apoftle, behold, all
things are become new. Judaifm, would
he fay, Judaifm, with all its burden, fome
ordinances and cuftoms, is fuperfeded by
the chriftian doctrine; the wall of feparation between the Jews and Heathens is
broken down; chriftianity has produced a
great and happy revolution of fentiments
and manners, in religion and worfhip, in
the

the whole state of mankind; it has done
much for the advancement of their perfection and happiness.

Let us, therefore, from these words,
consider the general advantage that christianity has procured to the human race in
general, and still procures; advantages
which even they who deny or doubt of the
divine origin of the christian doctrines,
must allow to be highly valuable and important.

We may reduce these advantages to four
chief heads. The first comprehends knowledge; the second, virtue; the third, tranquillity; and the fourth, the outward condition of men.

First, the cultivation of the human mind,
and the knowledge of truth in general,
has been improved and promoted by christianity among mankind. As christianity

does

does not, like the old heathen religion, confift in celebrations and ceremonies, in folemnities and facrifices, but in doctrines and moral precepts; fo muft it neceffarily have excited mankind, by degrees, to more reflection on invifible, fpiritual, and moral matters, on their mutual relation and con-nection with each other, on what they are at prefent, and what they will be hereafter; and thefe reflections muft, by degrees, have fpread themfelves among all ranks and conditions of men, which, till then, only the wife, as they were called, were in pof-feffion of. By this means the culture of the human mind, in general, has been very much promoted, and will in courfe of time continue to be more fo, as mankind pro-ceed to perceive how far chriftianity is from enfeebling the rights of found reafon, and how favourable it is, on the contrary, to the free inveftigation of truth. By this means many precepts of wifdom, much know-ledge, which were formerly looked upon

as

as the peculiar property of the philoso-
phers, are already incorporated into the
general mass of human knowledge; and
thus, by degrees, all that is useful and good
of this kind, together with the peculiar
doctrines of religion, will be a known and
serviceable treasure to every man, and be
delivered and accepted to the purpose of
acquiring wisdom and knowledge by every
man. Thus much, at least, is certain, that,
among none of the heathen nations, the
Greek and Roman not excepted, were there
such numbers of persons, of all ranks,
who reflected on their most important concerns, on God and religion, on morality
and virtue, on the end of their existence,
and their immortality, and by reflection
proceeded so far, as among the christians;
and, for this extraordinary circumstance, I
know of no consistent reason to be given,
but that of christianity itself. I will not
deny, that, considered as a predominant
religion, at certain times it has been as great

an-

an impediment to reflection and liberal in-
quiry as heathenifm ; and that, at times, it
has confifted, in regard of the generality of
its profeffors, in a blind implicit belief.
But I fpeak at prefent of the ·advantages.
we owe to chriftianity, confidered at large ;
and if it has not, at all times, and always
in the fame degree, been ʹproductive of
them by the fault of mankind, yet they
ftill fubfifted, and it is undeniable that we
are at prefent greatly indebted to its falu-
·tary influence.

Let it not be faid that we are chiefly
obliged to the writings of the antient fages
of Greece and Rome, and the general pub-
lication of them, for the cultivation of the
human mind, and the progrefs human
knowledge has made. If we examine the
matter thoroughly, we fhall find that even
the benefits we have obtained from that
quarter, and ftill may obtain, are all derived from chriftianity. I decry not the
writings

writings of thefe antient fages: I am fenfible to the beautiful, the true, and the
good they contain. But what has preferved
thefe writings to us, and prefented us with
them? Is it not chriftianity that has procured them to us, and, as it were, given us
them afrefh? How happened it that the
languages wherein thefe writings are compofed, and which were no longer fpoken
any where, were ftudied and purfued, but
becaufe the worfhip of feveral chriftians
was performed in them, and becaufe they
were the languages of their facred books?
Had it not been for this, would they not,
like many other antient languages, which
are only known to us by their names, have
fallen into complete oblivion, and, with the
treafures of wifdom they contain, have become a prey to all-devouring time?

But, if chriftianity be favourable to the
advancement of human fcience in general,
the knowledge of God and of religion in
parti-

particular has been much more benefited thereby. How widely has the doctrine of the eternity of God been diffeminated by chriftianity! Not only all chriftians of every fect and denomination, but even all mohammedans, who inhabit fo confiderable a part of the earth, and are probably ftill more numerous than the chriftians, are indebted for their belief of one true God, that firft principle of all real religion, to the chriftian revelation. And how important is this doctrine! By it alone the world becomes to us a perfect fyftem, wherein all things are moft intimately connected together, and tend to one and the fame great end. By this doctrine alone man is taught to know the Author of his exiftence, the Source of his felicity, the Supreme Object of his adoration, the Foundation of his hopes. Enlightened by this doctrine, he no longer confiders himfelf as a fatherlefs orphan, or as the offspring of blind chance, or groaning under the authority of feveral

powerful

powerful beings to him unknown, and at variance with each other. He knows from whom he fprings, on whom he depends, under whofe infpeĉtion he is, and will for ever be; and he has now a certain fixed point, in which all his thoughts, defires, endeavours, defigns, and hopes, unite as in their proper centre.

How greatly has the prevalence of idolatry been diminifhed in the world by chriftianity! and how many regions of it are freed from the tyrannical fway of fuperftition, and from the iron fceptre of cunning and felf-interefted priefts! and what flavifh notions, what tormenting uncertainty, what fears, what terrors, what childifh fentiments, what empty hopes and frivolous joys, muft debafe and perplex mankind, where the abominations of idolatry prevail! Calamities and horrors, from which chriftianity has redeemed millions of human creatures, and ourfelves among them; and

3 by

by their abolition has prepared the way for millions of mankind, and for us among them, to liberty, to peace of mind, to firm and generous principles ! That we are now no longer terrified at every uncommon appearance in nature ; that we no longer perceive, at every ftep we take, the prognoftications and figns of imminent misfortune or approaching danger ; that we are not continually obliged to be contriving new forms of facrifice and new modes of expiation ; that we are no longer in dread of the cafual neglect or imperfect obfervance of numberlefs rites and ceremonies ; that we do not take every adverfe event that befalls us for the vengeance of an enraged God ; that we do not allow ourfelves implicitly to be led by others, but dare to follow our own fentiments and feelings : for all thefe privileges and bleffings, we are indebted to the abolition of idolatry, and therefore to chriftianity. Though many fuperftitions may ftill prevail among chriftians, and for-

merly

merly many more than at prefent, yet we,
and with us many thoufands of our brethren, are freed from them by the influence
of chriftianity, and therein lie the fruitful
means for the total eradication of it from
among its confeffors; means which are continually coming forth into practice, and
allow us to hope for the moft glorious
effects.

And how much is the knowledge of this
only true God, and his relationfhip to us,
advanced and extended among mankind by
the doctrines of chriftianity! Every chriftian, that is not completely ignorant, confeffes and reveres the true God, not as a
being who, infinitely exalted above him,
ftands in no kind of connection with him;
but knows and reveres him as his Creator
and Preferver, as his Father and Benefactor,
as the Ruler and Judge of the world, as
the Obferver and Rewarder of human actions. And how prolific muft this conception

tion be among chriftians, who reflect more attentively upon it! how muft it furnifh them with the folution of a thoufand things which were before inexplicable myfteries to them! They difcover traces of the wif- dom, the power, and the goodnefs of this God, wherever they turn; they fee him every where acting for the benefit of all living creatures, and for their own; all things lead them back to him; and the thought of him fpreads light, and life, and joy, over the whole face of nature.

Certainly the reprefentations of what God is, of his perfections, and efpecially of what he is in regard to us, are, gene- rally fpeaking, even among perfons of the inferior ftations in life, more juft, more fa- tisfactory, and more adapted to promote virtue and happinefs, than they ever were among the heathen nations, not excepting even the majority of their wifeft men, or could be, by their mythology. What low, grofs,

grofs, and contemptible reprefentations did they make of their gods in general, of their difpofitions, of their actions, of their pleafures! what weakneffes, what paffions, what iniquities, were not afcribed to them! and how little was even the father of gods and men, as the Greeks and Romans ftyled their fupreme divinity, exempted from them! How much jufter are the notions diffufed by chriftianity, on this article, among mankind of every ftation, of every age, and of every profeffion! Indeed, even thefe conceptions are very imperfect, and muft remain fo, as finite man is not able to comprehend infinity. The beft conceptions, indeed, of many chriftians are mixed with various errors. But, with all thefe imperfections and failings, they are ftill incomparably better and worthier than theirs. What chriftian, however mode-rately informed, that does not know and believe that God is the moft holy, the moft perfect, the beft of beings; that he is al-

mighty, all-knowing, and every-where prefent, fupremely juft, and fupremely good;
that he cannot do evil, and never tempts any
man to wickednefs; that he loves virtue
and integrity above all things; that he abhors every fpecies of iniquity and fin; and
that there are no better means of pleafing
him, and of fecuring his favour, than by
doing juftice and loving mercy, and, like
him, to promote the good of mankind!
And are there not thoufands of men, at
prefent among the chriftians, for one among
the heathens, who raife themfelves to ftill
higher and more adequate reprefentations
of the Deity; who carefully feparate every
thing that is weak, human, and narrow,
from thefe reprefentations; who confider
and revere the Creator as a being affimi-
lated with every thing that is great, and
good, and beautiful, and perfect, inceffantly employed in beneficence, willing
and effecting nothing but felicity; who is
to be won by no outward tokens of reverence,

rence, to be foothed by no rites or offerings; who is infinitely fuperior to all human paffions, to all the emotions of wrath,
or partiality, or revenge; who requires no
flavifh dread of him from us, but only
filial reverence and love; and who is fupremely worthy of our moft ardent adoration, of our fincereft affection, of our moft
chearful obedience, and our firmeft confidence!

.   Add to this, proper knowledge of God,
the general and firm belief of our immortality, and the future remuneration, which
chriftianity, wherever it has been preached
and received, has fo deeply imprinted on
the hearts of men, and fo intimately interwoven with their whole courfe of reflection,
that even the moft violent attacks of infide-
lity cannot, with the generality, eradicate
or weaken it.   Confider, likewife, that this
belief inculcates fuch an immortality, and
fuch a remuneration, as is confequent upon

N 2   the

the moral conduct of men in this life, on
their virtues and their vices; and conclude,
from thence, how favourable this faith
muft, generally fpeaking, be to the amendment and repofe of mankind, and how
much more force it muft have to this effect
than the dark, uncertain, doubtful, falfe,
and immoral fignifications of this doctrine
which obtained in the heathen world, and
which, as it appears, were not much regarded by ordinary perfons, and were
looked upon by the wife as difficult and
inexplicable problems.

A fecond clafs of general advantages,
for which our thanks are due to chriftianity, relates to human virtue and integrity.
Thefe, upon the whole, have likewife
greatly gained thereby. Notions of virtue
are, in general, more juftly framed among
chriftians than they were among the heathens. Every one knows, that effential
virtue confifts neither in bodily ftrength,

nor

nor in the valour that braves all dangers;
neither in courage nor intrepidity in war, nor
in the great atchievements of heroes and
conquerors, commonly as deſtructive as renowned. Every one knows that it does
not conſiſt merely in abſtinence from groſs
and flagrant violations of order, or in particular actions, though juſt and good; but
that it comprehends the whole turn of
mind, and the whole ſeries of conduct;
that it is expreſſive of our intire moral
perfection; that we are viituous, when we
are and do all that we can be and do, according to our abilities, our vocation, and
our circumſtances, when our ſentiments and
behaviour are regulated by the will of God
and the injunctions of his laws. It is known
and received as a general principle, that
real virtue conſiſts not in the attachment
and affection to certain perſons, or to a particular nation, founded on contempt and
hatred towards the whole human race, but
in an enlarged deſire, and ſtrenuous endea-

N 3   vours,

vours, to promote the happiness of all mankind. And how much more adapted is this
conception of it, for which we are chiefly
indebted to chriftianity, to further and confirm the tranquillity, the fecurity, and the
welfare of human fociety, than that barbarous patriotic virtue, as it was called, fo
much accounted of in the old heathen
world, and which is ftill fo often extolled
by partial judges, to the detriment of
chriftian virtue! But particularly the filent
and domeftic virtues, the virtues of common life, whofe beneficial influence on the
public welfare is fo various and lafting,
have acquired a greater dignity by chriftianity; they have obtained the fo much
merited, but formerly fo much undifco-
vered, preference to the boafted heroic virtues, which, for the moft part, were founded on injuftice and violence.

The doctrine of virtue, among chriftians,
is clofely connected with the doctrine of
God

God and religion, and is therefore to every man, and especially to the inferior classes of mankind, much plainer, much more fixed, and much more forcible, than it could possibly be among the heathens. Among them, religion and virtue were two distinct things, not connected together; nay, frequently in direct opposition to each other. The heathens, that is, particular persons, or some sages among them, had a morality; but heathenism, or the heathenish religion, had none. Morals, therefore, rested intirely either on the natural sentiment of the difference between good and evil, which was debilitated and almost destroyed; or on philosophical investigations of the nature and connections of man and the material world, totally above the comprehension of the generality of their fellow citizens. Christianity, as well as Socrates, but in a far loftier sense, and in a much more general and effectual manner, has brought down true wisdom from heaven to the earth—

has

has reduced it to the underftanding and the heart of every man—has drawn it from the fchools of the learned, mixed it with common life, and, by uniting religion and morality together, has rendered eafy and important the knowledge of our nature and the practice of our duties.

How many motives, how many incitements to integrity and virtue, does this happy junction of morality with religion put the chriftian in poffeffion of, who is not totally ignorant or inattentive! He cannot avoid making fuch reflections as thefe on a thoufand occafions: God, my Creator and Preferver, my Benefactor, and my Judge, requires me to do this, and to abftain from the other. This he hath exprefsly commanded me; that he hath as exprefsly forbidden. If I do the one, he will blefs and reward me; if I do not abftain from the other, he will call me to account, and the confequence will be fatal. My life and

and my fortunes are both in his hand;
both are dependant on his grace and favour; without them I cannot hope for
fuccefs, and nothing can fhield me from
the effects of his difpleafure. From how
many irregularities muft thefe reflections
not reftrain him, though they fhould not
be altogether juft! though they fhould be
accompanied by many erroneous conceptions! and to how many proper, good,
and generous actions muft they not incite
him! how much muft confcientioufnefs,
integrity, and fidelity in fecret, be promoted thereby!

Both hiftory and experience uniformly
confirm thefe good effects of chriftianity, in
regard to the moral conduct of mankind.
It is not to be denied, that many unnatural
and deftructive vices, which heathenifm to-
lerated and favoured, are now, even in
places where, by means of the chriftian
doctrine, they are not intirely eradicated
from

from amongſt its confeſſors, are now brand-
ed with ſo much infamy and diſgrace, that
they are no longer allowed to be named.
It is not to be denied, that, on the whole,
more integrity and honour, more fidelity
and confidence in commerce, and all deal-
ings between man and man, prevail among
chriſtians than amongſt the moſt poliſhed
nations that are not chriſtians.   It is not to
be denied, that the ſentiments of general
philanthropy and beneficence, and the indications of them, are far more frequent
and effective among them than ever they
were among the heathens.   The eſtabliſh-
ment and ſupport of ſo many hoſpitals, ſo
many inſtitutions for the maintenance of
orphans, for the comfort of the poor and
the ſick, of which we find ſcarcely any
traces among the heathens, are ſpeaking
examples of it.   In general, without partiality, we have a perfect right to maintain,
that among chriſtian nations, taken at large,
the knowledge of duty and virtue, a hatred
of

of wickednefs, and a love of goodnefs, and therefore their morality, is greater and more general, the reverence for the Deity and his laws more operative, the confciences of men more tender and delicate, and, in particular, the mild and focial virtues are far more common than they ever were among the people of any nation, that we know of, before the coming of Chrift.

A third clafs of general advantages, for which we are indebted to chriftianity, comprehends the tranquillizing of the human mind, and the fixing of their hopes. How confiderably have thefe, which are fuch effential parts of chriftianity, been gainers by its peculiar doctrines of Providence, and the Divine Government of the world, and the forgivenefs of fins, of the immortality of the foul, and of the life to come! The heathen, at leaft, among the Greeks and Romans, regarded his divinities either as idle beings, totally unconcerned about the

affairs

affairs of mortals, or as felfifh, partial, and
capricious, eafy to be provoked, and hard
to be appeafed. He knew not what affinity
he had to them, and what he was to fear
from their difpleafure, or to expect from
their favour. He muft confole himfelf
with the abfolute neceffity of gods and
men, with a blind and inflexible fate. On
the other hand, the chriftian, the unlearned
as well as the learned, the pooreft day-
labourer as well as the exalted amongft
the people, the chriftian is acquainted with
truths which have quite a different influence
on the repofe of his mind. There is, thus
can he reflect on all occafions, and thus
does he in fact very often think—There is
a Being fupremely wife, and fupremely
good, who is interefted about us all, whofe
creatures and children we are, who loves
and provides for us all. Nothing can happen without his will; and God, the All-
merciful, wills ever the beft. Nothing is
impoffible to him; he knows how to deliver

ver from death. To them that love him,
all things muft produce advantage. If he
be for us, none can be againft us. His
power is mighty in weaknefs. He will not
allow us to be tempted above what we are
able to bear. How much do thefe and the
like reflections lighten the hardeft toils, alleviate the greateft indigence, and mitigate
the fevereft afflictions, to many thoufands of
chriftians! How much courage and confidence do they give them in misfortunes
and perils! If we frequented the cottages
of the poor, the dwellings of the lower
classes of men, and made ourfelves acquainted with their habitual manner of
thinking, we fhould be convinced how
much comfort and tranquillity the chriftian
doctrine affords them all, almoft without
exception, as they receive and believe it in
fimplicity of heart; and are thereby free
from all the doubts with which the wife,
as they are called, are perpetually tormented; intirely repofing on what the fcrip-
tures

ture tells them, and conftantly fuppofing
God particularly employed in their concerns, and in the difpofition of their fortunes; and then we fhall rightly judge of
the advantage the chriftians muft have, in
this refpect likewife, over all the moft civilized nations that were or are not chriftian.

How much more eafily may the chriftian,
oppreffed by the fenfe of his fins and the
terror of punifhment, quiet his mind here-
upon, than any other man who finds himfelf in the fame fituation, but knows not
the chriftian doctrine! The chriftian
knows, and knows it with affurance, that
God is inclined to pity, and to fpare; that
he will forgive the contrite and converted
finner all his delinquencies without exception, and remit the penalty due to tranf-
greffion. He knows, and knows with certainty, what, in this refpect, he has to do;
he has no need to confider, with anxious
uncertainty, what multitudes of offerings,
what

3

what coftly prefents, what myftical atone-
ments and expiations, will procure his pardon, or what feverities of penance; but fo
foon as he draws nigh to his Creator and
Judge with an upright heart, abhors and
forfakes his wicked habits, and, effectually
determined on a better conduct, holds true
to his purpofe, he may immediately promife himfelf the favour of the Moft High,
and his heart condemns him no more.
What a healing and reviving balm muft
thefe chriftian doctrines have poured into
the wounded confciences and tortured
hearts of thoufands and thoufands, who
muft otherwife have become a prey to the
horrors of defpair!

We may advance the fame thing in regard to the dread of death, and the hope
of a better life. Though the fage of heathenifm, with a perplexed and doubting
fpirit, or in the gloomy expectation of
utter extinction, faw death approach him;
though

though the greateft number of them met
this ghaftly tyrant either with a recklefs
infenfibility, or with a fpirit ftruggling between darknefs and light, between fear and
hope ; yet chriftians, in general, being firmly perfuaded of their immortality, and the
eternal life that awaits them after death,
form jufter conceptions of the future ftate,
can more eafily, and with greater certainty,
promife themfelves a better portion there
than they have had on earth ; meet their diffolution, therefore, with far greater calmnefs
and comfort ; and many thoufands of them
actually tread the path of death without
difmay, and in the joyous, indubitable expectation of an everlafting continuation of
exiftence, a glorious, interminable, and
ever-increafing felicity : infallible argu-
ments, that leave us no room to doubt
that there not only may be, but that there
actually is, among chriftians, far more comfort and hope than was ever to be found
among the heathens.

Recollect,

Recollect, at the same time, for we cannot here finish the subject, recollect the multitudes of institutions and means for promoting knowledge, virtue, and the peace of mankind, that owe their origin to christianity.

Think on the numerous schools, erected in all the towns and most of the villages in christian countries, and which, considered as schools of religion and morality, were wholly unknown among the heathens, at least among the Greeks and Romans, and likewise among our anceftors, the antient inhabitants of our island. Defective and illiberal as the generality of these schools, in more than one respect, may be, yet children are there brought to the knowledge of the only true God, and disciplined in his fear, instructed in their duties, cautioned against all finfulnefs and vice, and incited to virtue by various ways.

Reflect on the paftoral office every where introduced into the chriftian church, devoted to the inftruction, the encouragement, and the comfort of individuals of every condition, age, and fex ; an inftitution peculiar in its kind, and which certainly a Socrates, a Plato, a Cicero, and a Confucius, would have admired as the moft excellent and beneficial of all others, if they could have feen it in their days. Let this appointment be ever fo much abufed, let the delivery of the chriftian doctrines be never fo faulty ; yet the conveyance of inftruction in the moft important doctrines of religion and virtue, in fo public a manner, in fuch frequent returns, and often with the moft intimate fenfation and conviction, muft infinitely more contribute to the amelioration and repofe of mankind than all the folemnities and ceremonies of the heathens were ever able to do. Take this likewife into the account, that all thefe advantages, inftitutions,

tutions, and eftablifhments, are fo conftituted in the very nature of them, that they
cannot fail, by degrees, of becoming common, and of obtaining a certain degree of
perfection and actual influence ; and that
they are even now becoming conftantly,
and with no flow piogreffion, more perfect
and productive than they have hitherto
been : and thus it is an undeniable truth,
that we, and all mankind in general, are
under no ordinary obligation to chriftianity.

There are ftill a variety of other confiderable advantages for which we ftand indebted to the influence of this heavenly
doctrine, and which relate in great meafure to the outward condition of man. We
muft now, however, confine ourfelves to a
flight indication of them : that polyga-
my, for example, that fertile fource of
depopulation, of effeminacy and domeftic
mifery, is abolifhed ; that the inhuman,
barbarous cuftom of expofing children, on

account

account of some accidental infirmity, or
because they were disagreeable or burden-
some to their parents, and giving them up
to unavoidable ruin, is abhorred by all
men; that slavery, that unjustifiable degra-
dation of human nature, as it formerly obtained among the Greeks and Romans, and
other nations of antiquity, is, at least in
christian Europe, much diminished; that,
by the strenuous exertions of generous and
noble-minded men, we may entertain the
pleasing hope that it will, ere long, be held
in equal detestation by the inhabitants of
the different provinces in America as it is
with us; that laws and customs, with all
their allowed imperfections and inconsist-
ences, are still, in general, milder and more
humane; that war, in many respects, is
carried on with less cruelty and devastation;
that the conquered are spared, and neither
deprived of their lives nor their liberty;
that the sentiment of the moral dignity of
man, the acknowledgement of the natural

I   equality

equality of the human race, and a due regard for each other among individuals,
are underſtood and felt, and are every day
becoming more univerſal and effective;
that many corrupt paſſions, deſtructive to
ſociety, as revenge, ambition, tyranny, are
reſtrained to narrower bounds, and meet
with more powerful controul, or are directed to a nobler channel: for all theſe
advantages we are indebted, though indeed
not altogether and alone, but in a great
meaſure, to chriſtianity, and its influence
on the general opinion and manners of its
confeſſors; and ſurely the peace, the ſecu-
rity, the welfare of ſocial life, muſt be
much improved thereby.

So many, ſuch great advantages, in reſpect to knowledge, to virtue and integrity,
to our tranquillity and hopes, and our ex-
ternal welfare, do we owe to the doctrine of
Jeſus, whoſe appearance in the world we
this day commemorate. And muſt not the

conſidera-

confideration of thefe advantages, which
we all poffefs and enjoy, infpire us with
gladnefs at our felicity, and with gratitude
to God, the Author and Giver of it? Yes,
chriftian feftivals are real days of rejoicing,
but with a joy that relates particularly to
the bounty of God, our Father in heaven,
who allows us to feel the whole worth of
his parental protection and love, and im-
preffes our hearts with gratitude towards
him. Let us, then, excite thefe joys within
us, and endeavour to render them poignant
and lively by reflection. To this end, let
us tranfport ourfelves, in fpirit, into the
times of heathenifm, vifit the temple of
the gods, reprefent to ourfelves the frivolous worfhip their adorers paid them, and
the fuperftitious terrors that furrounded
thefe abodes of impofture; let us lament
over the far greater ignorance, wickednefs,
and comfortlefs condition, that formerly
prevailed among mankind; let us bewail
the miferable fate of the nations, who blind-

ly

ly followed their fightlefs guides, who proftrated themfelves before wood and ftone; who lived, as it were, without God, and without hope, in the world, and among whom alfo our forefathers were; and then compare our happier condition with theirs, and render due honour to chriftianity, by which this beneficial revolution was brought about.

Or, if we cannot make this comparifon, from a deficiency of hiftorical information, we need not go fo far from our own times, and from the prefent prevailing fentiments; let us, however, at leaft, reflect what condition our knowledge, our virtue, our hope, our outward welfare, the fecurity and peace of fociety, would be in, had we been bereaved of the advantage we have now confidered as the fruit of chriftianity. In all probability, we fhould then have lain buried in the thickeft darknefs of ignorance and fuperftition; we fhould

have

have been blind idolaters, miferable flayes, dupes or impoftors, the fport of our pro-penfities and paffions; fearful, hopelefs, wretched mortals. Now are we children of light; men who know their Creator, their duties, and the end of their creation; worfhipers of the true God, comforted by his providence, by his grace, by the ex-pectation of a better and an eternal life; members of a civilized fociety, where vice is detefted, where virtue is efteemed and prized; where, upon the whole, much in-tegrity, much philanthropy, much truth and confidence, is actually to be found. How happy, then, is it for us that Jefus appeared on the earth, and promulgated his doctrine! What thanks do we owe to him and his heavenly Father, who gave him to us for our teacher and deliverer!

And how much happier may we ftill become, by employing his doctrine aright! We muft not be fatisfied with the general

advan-

advantages to all nations and languages. We muft ftrive to reach the higheft perfection and happinefs, to which it is adapted to lead us. We muft, therefore, continually improve in the knowledge of this excellent doctrine; apply it more feduloufly to ourfelves; allow ourfelves to be more and more animated by its fpirit, and ftudy to think and live in a more chriftian manner. We muft follow its directions, to the obtaining of felicity, with a chearful and intire dedition of our hearts, and obferve all its precepts with unremitted attention. Thus fhall we endeavour to become, by its means, intirely free, thoroughly wife, and perfectly virtuous, perfectly and eternally bleffed!

Chriftmas-day,
    1787.

E S T I-

ESTIMATE XVII,

THE

VALUE

OF THE

HUMAN SOUL.

We are the offspring of God.

Acts xvii. 29.

———————

THE

VALUE

OF THE

HUMAN SOUL.

R IGHTLY to fix the value of things,
not to fet more by them, and not to
beftow on them a greater degree of affection than they deferve; to connect the prefent with the future, and, in drawing our
conclufions, to look not only at the former
but alfo at the latter; never to lofe fight of
our grand defign, and to regard and ufe all
other things only as means to the advancement of it: this is the character of the
wife and prudent. To judge of externals
by the firft impreffion they make on our
fenfes, which is often a very fallacious one;

to

to treat empty trifles as matters of great moment, and important affairs as contemptible trifles; to follow blind inftincts, or corrupted paffions, in the choice of the objects of our love and efteem; to facrifice a great future fortune to a prefent momentary pleafure, or transient advantage; to take the means for the end, or to live in the world without a determinate plan upon a bare capital: this is the character of a fool. But who is that fage, if it be not the chriftian, who thinks and acts conformably to his heavenly calling? Who is this fool, if it be not the fenfual man, who follows his inordinate defires, and lofes heaven for the goods of the earth? The former, the true chriftian, holds all that is terreftrial and tranfient for what it actually is, and will hereafter be; and this moderates his affection towards it, and renders the lofs of it by no means intolerable: the latter, the mere fenfnal man, feeks his whole happinefs in earthly things; and, if they

they chance to be ravished from him, he thinks himself cast into the lowest depth of misery, as indeed he is, since he has nothing left to compensate the loss. The former directs his desires to the worthiest things; his whole heart is devoted to God and religion, to virtue and friendship: the latter bestows his whole love and esteem on such things as are unworthy of them, and hostile to his vocation. The former knows that he has an immortal spirit, and all his endeavours tend to render that nobler part of his being more perfect, and more fitted for that sublimer state he is hastening to enter: the latter forgets, as it were, that he has a reasonable soul, that is to live for ever, and confines his cares to his outward condition, and to that which flatters his senses. The former lives for eternity, and considers his proceedings here as preparatory to it: the latter limits all his reflections, desires, and views to the short moment of his earthly pilgrimage, and loses

sight

fight of the term to which it leads. After
this contraſt of the temper and conduct of
the true chriſtian, with the temper and conduct of the diforderly man, can we for a
moment doubt that the former purſues the
dictates of wifdom, and that the latter betrays the greateſt folly? Whence, however, proceeds this difference in their character and conduct? The chriſtian under-
ſtands and feels the whole value, the high
dignity, the important appointment of his
foul; he frequently reflects upon it; he
compares what he is, and does, impartially
with what he ought to be, and to do; and
ſtrives to conduct himſelf according to his
knowledge. The other, on the contrary,
allows all this to efcape him, and judges
and acts, in the generality, and the moſt important of cafes, as if he belonged to an
inferior order of beings. Of fo much confequence is it, that we fhould frame to
ourſelves right notions of the value and
excellency of our foul, and that thefe notions

tions fhould have an effective influence on our conduct. To this end, let us confider the high value, the excellency and dignity of the human foul : but let us, likewife, attend to the behaviour that is fitting for fuch noble, fuch highly favoured creatures as we are. Thefe two confiderations com- pofe the matter of my prefent attempt, and they are certainly of a nature to merit your utmoft attention.

The nature and origin of the human foul, its great capacities and powers; what God has done, and ftill continues to do for its prefervation, and the advancement of its happinefs ; its appointment, and its fu- ture lot : all thefe proclaim it of exalted worth, and fet it beyond all doubt to re- flecting creatures.

How lofty is the origin of the human foul ! How far, in this refpect, does it ex- cel the body ! This is formed of the duft :

Vol. II.   P   it

it is produced by generation. It lies concealed in other terreftrial bodies, and its developement is occafioned by mortal man. The foul, as the Scripture fays, is of divine defcent, is the offspring of God. God is, in a peculiar fenfe, her Creator and Father, as he is the Creator and Father of fuperior fpirits: fhe is, therefore, related to thofe exalted beings. Yes, fhe bears the imprefs of him that made her; and even the ftate of meannefs, and of moral corruption, wherein fhe is at prefent, cannot totally efface the glorious refemblance. Her reafon is a ray of his unbounded intellect; her freedom and power is derived from his unlimited and conftantly efficient might; her love to what is beautiful and good, to order and perfection, her friendly and beneficent emotions, are emanations of his pure holinefs, of his eternal and unalterable benignity.

Her

Her fpiritual nature, raifed, fo far above all that we difcern about us, and in connection with us, bears witnefs alfo of its excellency, and of her high defcent. She tells us exprefsly that fhe is not of the earth, but that fhe came from heaven. Had we already no plain and clear conception of the nature of our foul, fhould we fay, that, as far as we could difcover, fhe is a fimple effence, it would be much the fame as faying that fhe is, not like matter compofed of parts : then our reflection, as well as our feeling, would inform us that fhe is fomewhat wholly different from the body fhe inhabits, and is far more excellent than it. The body continues not a fingle moment in the fame ftate in which it was before. It is continually undergoing various alterations, which, imperceptible as in part they may be, yet, taken together, are very confiderable. It is conftantly lofing numberlefs little particles, which are as conftantly, by means of air, of food, and

drink,

drink, replaced by others; and thus, in the courfe of a few years, our body is, as it were, totally renewed. But, amidft all thefe revolutions of its groffer fhell, the foul remains invariably the fame. She is confcious, at every period of time, that fhe is exactly what fhe was in any previous portion of her life. She can connect the paft, the prefent, and the future together, though the paft be long fince paft, and for the future there be no reafon difcoverable in the material world. She begets reflection, fhe makes conclufions, fhe exhibits powers, which not only have nothing fimilar to what we term magnitude, figure, folidity, and movement, but are contradictory to all thefe properties of matter. All her ideas, diverfified and numberlefs as they may be, concentrate themfelves, as it were, in one point, which we muft necef-farily reprefent as indivifible. She is therefore of a quite different, of a far more permanent and unchangeable nature than our body,

body, and all the other things that fall under the perception of our fenfes.

Hence likewife it is, that the well-being of the foul depends not fo much on the outward circumftances in which fhe finds herfelf, as on her own moral frame : fo as that fhe may be wretched in the poffeffion of the moft brilliant advantages of life, and be fad amidft the free ufe of all the fources of joy that human fociety can open, if error, paffion, and vice, fhed darknefs and difmay upon her : fo can fhe, likewife, be contented in the want of all the goods of fortune, and comforted under the burden of fevere afflictions, if the knowledge of truth, the confcioufnefs of innocence, the fentiment of her dignity, and the profpect of the future world, infpire her with light and reft, with hope and affurance. She can maintain her nobility in the loweft ftation, her freedom in the bonds of flavery, her brightnefs at the fight of death and

P 3

cor-

corruption : fhe can preferve her virtue under .all temptations, her fortitude in all
dangers, and her greatnefs under all op-
preffions. She foars above every thing
earthly and vifible ; preffes by meditation
into the very abode of the perfected juft ;
gets a foretafte of their purer joys, and
looks down from this eminence on all that
is tranfient and vain with compaffion and
contempt. Her perfection and happinefs
repofe on fuch properties, views, fenfations,
and aptitudes, as no changes of fortune
can affect; which fhe cannot lofe, though
heaven and earth fhould pafs away. How
excellent, then, muft be the nature of the
human foul ! how valuable muft thefe advantages render it, beyond all that is material !

Caft, fecondly, a look at her capacities
and powers, and you will ftill plainer perceive her excellency, and her value. How
noble is the employment of the human
mind !

mind ! how great the perfection of which
it is fufceptible ! how many great and aftonifhing things is man able to execute with
it ! he thinks, and is confcious of it. He
forms to himfelf clear reprefentations of
the things that are without him, and can
increafe the number of thefe images without end. He compares his ideas with one
another, judges of their harmony or their
contradiction, and combines them in thoufands of various ways. He proceeds from
known things to unknown, from the eafy
to the difficult; adopts principles, draws
conclufions, concatenates thefe conclufions
together, and is ever opening new profpects
in the unlimited regions of truth that lies
before him. Would he difmifs his ideas,
they fly from his prefence : are they obfcure, he fpreads a new light upon them :
are they vanifhed away, he calls them back.
With his underftanding, man 'retraces his
own capacities and powers, and obferves
the rife, the progrefs, and the varied com-

bination

bination of his reflections, his propenfities, and his defires. By means of his underftanding, man rules over all the creatures of the earth; knows how to reftrain their ftrength, and over-rule their fubtlety, by prudence, and to facilitate by their fervice the moft difficult tafks; and the whole inanimate and irrational creation is rendered fubfervient to his profit and pleafure. By his underftanding, when Providence has allotted him an exalted ftation among his brethren, he comprehends the multifarious and complicated concerns of intire kingdoms and ftates; judges of the ftrength and the weaknefs of every particular diftrict, and of his affinity to the whole; is vigilant and provident for the benefit of all; knows how to connect the moft different capacities, the moft oppofite inclinations, defigns, and motions of his fubjects with each other, to keep them in their due equilibrium, and to turn them all to the advancement of one and the fame great end;

end; enlightens and animates millions of men by the radiance he diffufes around him, and governs them fo, that, in their fovereign, they revere the kindeft of fa- thers. He proceeds ftill farther with his intellect: by unremitted reflection, and by the help of a refearching mind, he dives into the fecrets of nature; penetrates the latent caufes, properties, and effects of things; fees and admires the wifdom and art difcernible in the fmalleft infect no lefs than in the ftructure of the world, and, from obfervations of what are in and for themfelves apparently of little import, dif- covers the univerfal law by which the largeft of the heavenly bodies roll. With his underftanding man lifts himfelf from earth to heaven, paffes the orbs and the diftances of the ftars, arranges them in claffes, adjufts their dimenfions, weighs their folidity, and feeks and finds the place where they have ftood for thoufands of years, and where they may ftand for ages

to

to come. Nay, with his understanding man soars to the knowledge of the Great First Cause of all things, to the knowledge of him who is the Creator and Lord of him and the universe, who is Beauty and Perfection itself, before whose grandeur and glory suns and worlds are nothing. Even the infinite attributes of this most Exalted Being are not absolutely hidden from him : he sees them resplendent in all his works, and studies his eternal will from the constitutions and arrangements he has established in nature.

And who can settle the boundaries of the imagination and memory of the human soul! The former traverses the immense region of creation, far swifter than light; ranges from one solar, from one planetary system to another; forms new worlds to itself; connects the past with the present, and pierces to the remotest futurity: the latter, the memory, can restore to its pris-
tine

fine difpofition and arrangement all that
we have ever felt, all that we have ever
thought, and of which no trace remains
without us; it can ftore up unnumbered
ideas of the moft diffimilar things, without confufion or mixture, for our future
ufe; it can contain, within itfelf, the
whole circle of arts and fciences, all that
ancient and modern hiftory comprehends
of remarkable tranfactions, of the inventions and difcoveries of mankind, ever
augmenting this enormous ftock of knowledge, and at all times delivering to us
whatever is beft adapted to our prefen
purpofe.

With what faculties, farther, is the human foul endowed! The faculty by which,
of its mere will, not as an effect of a natural and irrefiftible infiinct, but from free
choice, with complete confcioufnefs, and
to wifely directed aims, the moft diverfified
movements in our body, and by means
whereof

whereof a thoufand revolutions, in the objects without us, inftantaneoufly and infallibly take place, and at the command
whereof as fuddenly and certainly ceafe :
this power is an image of the Omnipotence
that calls that which is not into being, and
orders that to pafs away which is to exift
no more. It is a power that we know not
how to explain, but which undoubtedly
has fomething godlike in it, and exalts
man far above the inanimate and the irrational creation; a faculty that, likewife,
muft have a great and beneficial influence
on our moral conduct, if we ftudied to
exert it with greater confideration, and
learnt to apply it aright.

In fhort, how far may it not carry the
human foul in moral perfection! She is
not neceffitated to follow a blind and irrefiftible inftinct : fhe determines herfelf :
fhe acts from difcernment and free election,
by knowledge and argument. She knows
the

the femblances of good and evil from what
is actually fo, and how to diftinguifh them
apart; and how to bring the remoteft confequences of things into confideration,
when needful to her in drawing her conclufions. She is fufceptible of the nobleft
fentiments, and capable of the moft mag-
nanimous actions. Has the defire of pleafing
God, and of accomplifhing his will, has
the love of truth and virtue, once got the
afcendency in her, then may fhe withftand
and repel the ftrongeft incitements to fin,
either outward or inward. She can chearfully facrifice either renown or might, either
riches or honour, either quiet or fortune,
either health or life, to her duty. To refemble God, her heavenly Father, in juftice
and beneficence, to copy him ever more
clofely, and to render herfelf ever more
capable of nearer communion with him, is
the ultimate object of her endeavours and
defires. This exalted aim fhe purfues with
an undeviating ardour; readily renounces

every

every thing that would turn her afide; becomes conftantly wifer and better, and never ceafes from ftriving after higher degrees of perfection. What a value, what a dignity muft the human foul poffefs, adorned as fhe is with fuch capacities and powers, and capable of fuch a high degree, of fo inceffant an elevation of knowledge and virtue!

It is true, that even the human foul, from whofe capacities and powers we conclude of her excellence, has likewife her weak fide; and were I to deny it, or endeavour to hide it from you, the experience of all mankind, of every age, would charge me with falfhood and infincerity. Yes, we all but too frequently experience how eafily our foul faints under the preffure of intenfe application; how fuddenly fhe is precipitated from the heights to which fhe had climbed, and how often fhe fatigues herfelf in vain to fcan and explore them. We all

all but too much experience how eafily we
are feduced into error, how quickly we
fuffer ourfelves to be hurried away by violent paffions; how often we accept the
femblance of a matter for its actual fub-
ftance; and how difficult it is for us to re-
gain the path of truth and virtue, when
once we have deviated from it. All of us
experience but too much, that, at prefent,
we are ftill furrounded by great darknefs
and uncertainty; that our knowledge is but
imperfect; that, in moft of our aims, we
walk by faith, and not by fight; and that,
in fine, the nobleft capacities of our nature
can only be carried to a certain degree of
perfection on earth, by the fmalleft proportion of mankind. But be upon your guard,
that, from thefe experiences, you draw no
conclufions detrimental to the value and
dignity of the human foul. Confider under what adverfe circumftances fhe lives
and acts in this world. Confider how much
fhe is oppreffed by the corruption of fin;
how

how much fhe is confined by the irregularities and infirmities of the body; how
much fhe is molefted and impeded in her
functions by the wants and affairs of this
life, which demand the greateft part of our
time, and the principal exertions of our
powers; and how often her fire is even re-
preffed in education; and reprefent to yourfelves what fhe will be, when thefe circumftances fhall be changed, thefe impediments
removed, and fhe finds herfelf in another
and a better world. Then will fhe firft
fhew herfelf in her intire vigour, and, if
we at prefent pay a becoming attention to
her illuminations and falvation, will proceed with hafty fteps from one degree of
perfection to another. Here, according to
the wife conftitution that God has fettled,
fhe neither can nor ought to be fo perfect
as by her nature fhe is adapted to become;
and hereby fhe lofes no more of her worth
and excellency, than the diamond lofes of its
intrinfic value by not being cut and polifhed.
But,

But, it may be faid, what are thefe faculties and powers of the human foul, let them be as great as they may, when compared with the powers and faculties of fuperior Beings? Indeed, my pious hearer, when I confider the immeafurable magnitude of the univerfe; when I reflect how probable it is, that we occupy but one of the loweft places among the intelligent creatures of God; when I ruminate on the diftance between mankind and the higheft order of fpirits, which may be as great, and probably much greater than the diftance between the acuteft human mind and that of the fimpleft infant; at fuch times I am loft in my own reflections; it then appears to me as if the afcribing of fuch value to the human foul as I am ufed to give it, were nothing more than a fuggeftion of over-weening pride. In thofe moments comes Jefus to my aid. He teaches me what God, the Creator of fpirits, has done for the human foul; and this frees me from all doubt that it muſt have a great value in his ſight, who alone can infallibly judge of the value of things. I ſhall not, at preſent, obſerve how much the wiſdom and goodneſs of God is revealed in the ſtructure of the body which the ſoul inhabits; how curiouſly all the properties and parts of it are adapted to its inſtruction; and how plainly all the methods of his providence tend to the advancement of its perfection. I ſhall only now remind you of the divine information we acquire by the goſpel of Chriſt. What we learn therein of the love of God towards man muſt neceſſarily confer upon our nature a quite peculiar, an inexpreſſible dignity. Yes, when I contemplate that love as the love of a father for his children, that it has ordained us to the greateſt felicity, I can no longer doubt that the human ſoul is precious in his ſight. Then every heſitation ariſing from my reflections on the immenſity of the kingdom of God, on the count-

leſs

lefs multitude of his adorers, and on the inconfiderable ftation I fill amongft them, vaniſhes away from my mind. Then I recover from the illufion into which the confideration of his infinite greatnefs, and my own infignificancy, had thrown me. I am ſenfible to the whole value, the honour, and the felicity of being his child, of bearing his likenefs, and of being the brother of Jefus.

Figure to yourfelves, laftly, from the worth and excellency of your fouls, what their future appointment and lot muft be. This reflection muft already have arifen in your minds from the foregoing confiderations, that our foul is not, here, what by its nature it may and ought to be ; that its capacities and powers are far too great and noble to be completely difplayed in the prefent ftate of weaknefs ! And may we not thence venture to conclude, that the God who cannot poffibly fail in his defigns, and

Q 2   who

who imparts to his creatures no faculty
they never can employ, has not formed our
foul for this terreftrial fcene alone, that
this is but the firft and loweft ftep in the
fcale of its exiftence, that it is appointed
to a continually advancing, to an eternal
elevation? And muft we not draw this conclufion from what God has done for our
foul? Would he, who is wifdom itfelf,
who always exactly proportions the means
to his ends, would he have made fuch
great preparatives, fuch difpofitions, to our
natural and moral perfection, if he had
only produced us that we might pafs a few
years of more fenfible than rational life,
and then return to nothing? How! God
has made me capable of knowing him, of
revering him, of loving him, of feeking
my whole felicity in him; and I am to lofe
this capacity, from which I have a right to
promife myfelf fo much, which infpires
me with fo ardent a defire after a clofer
communion with this glorious Being; I am
to

to lofe it in death! No; God cannot
deftroy creatures whom he has endowed
with fuch faculties, and favoured fo highly
befides; and, if He cannot deftroy them,
then are they fafe from all deftruction. If
thefe conclufions, Sirs, be not fufficiently
forcible to convince you of this, then take
the inftructions of chriftianity thereupon:
they chafe away all darknefs and uncertainty from over it. Enlightened by the
light of chriftianity, we affuredly know
that our fouls fhall not die, that they fhall
live for ever, that they fhall exchange this
world hereafter for a better. There will
they unfold all their faculties and powers,
and rife to the higheft degree of activity
and ftrength. There will they proceed
from one ftep of knowledge to another,
from virtue to fuperior virtue, from happinefs to fupreme felicity, and nothing will
impede them in their progrefs. Glorious
arrangement! happy portion! For ever
fhall we live and act, for ever be more per-

Q 3   fect

fect and, happy, and for ever make nearer
approaches to God Moft High. Then
will our nature appear in the full difplay
of its dignity, in all its magnificence and
grandeur.

Behold, O man, the nobility of thy origin, the greatnefs of thy capacities! how
much God has done for thee! and 'how
exalted thy vocation is! Thy foul is of
divine defcent; it is capable of an ever-
increafing perfection; it is of immortal duration. O, praife thy Creator! let all that
is within thee extol his name! Feel thy
worth; forget not thy dignity; learn to
prize thyfelf, and think and act in proportion to thy value. Rejoice in thy happinefs, and be always rendering thyfelf more
fit for it by wifdom and virtue. But fhudder likewife at the mifery, at the incon-
ceiveable mifery, of which this natural ex-
celiency makes thee fufceptible, and fhun
the way that leads thereto, the way of vice,
which

which degrades thee, which hurls thee
from the throne which thou art ordained
to fill, and renders thee a flave.

O, how much are fenfual and earthly-
minded men to be pitied, who never rife
above vifible things, never ferioufly reflect
on the privileges granted them by God, on
the perfection and glory to which he has
called them; who are infenfible to their
nobleft powers, or mifapply them to vo-
luptuoufnefs, to unrighteoufnefs, and fin;
who are, as it were, all matter, and think
they live for no other purpofe than to fatif-
fy their corporeal wants, to abandon themfelves to fenfual gratifications, or to accu-
mulate unprofitable treafures! How can
they imagine that, for this end, God has fo
far exalted them above the beafts of the
earth, that to this end he has ufed fo many
extraordinary means for their deliverance,
and their falvation, or that in thefe purfuits
they fhall reach the end for which they

Q 4 were

were created! How can they boaft of, what is indeed the higheft boaft of man, that they are honoured with the image of God, and that they may be conftantly drawing nearer to this giorious Being, and ever gaining a clofer refemblance of him! No; they belye their quality; they debafe themfelves to an inferior clafs of beings; they defeat the great defigns their Maker has upon them; they prefer darknefs to light, flavery to freedom, a merely fenfual and animal life to one that is heavenly and divine. They fpurn the exalted, the ever-lafting felicity of which their nature is ca-pable, from them with contempt. Yet this is not all: they thus are preparing for themfelves punifhments, which will be fo much the heavier as the properties are more excellent which God has beftowed upon them, and which they abufe. This ye may do, O foolifh men; ye may weaken, degrade, and difgrace your foul, by folly and vice; ye may render it totally incapable

of

of the favour of God, and the blifs of the
future world ; ye may beguile it, and hide
your fhame and your mifery from yourfelves; but kill it you cannot : it is immortal : it will live for ever. It will wake
from its illufions in another ftate,; and then
will it feel the whole weight of the fhame
and mifery you lay upon it. Then will
you experience, to your extreme affright,
the truth of what the Saviour fays, that it
will profit a man nothing to have gained
the whole world, if he lofe his own foul.
Lamentable profpects! dreadful expectations! O ftrive to put your foul into a
better frame, ere that great day arrive
which fhall determine your future lot.
Raife yourfelves from the earth ; rend
yourfelves from the dominion of fordid
pleafures. Avail yourfelves of the gracious difpofitions God has made, by Chrift,
for the redemption of our fouls. Seek
from him, and his doctrine, that light
which can enlighten you, that power
which

which can improve and fanctify you, that comfort which can fave and blefs you. Accuftom yourfelves to confider and to judge of every thing by its analogy with the futurity that awaits you, and purfue fuch a courfe as is fuitable to the excellency of your nature.

Let the confideration of this excellency of the human foul inftruct and comfort you, ye poor and low among the people, whom neither riches, nor illuftrious defcent, nor exalted ftations, procure any regard. Let it infpire you, not with pride, but with a generous confidence, a lively fentiment of your inherent dignity. Let it teach you contentednefs in your condition. Let thefe confiderations ferve as means for fecuring you from all bafe fentiments, and all mean behaviour. That which really exalts mankind above the other creatures, what renders them capable of fuch great perfection and happinefs, is common to you with the

mightieft

mightieft of the earth, with princes and with kings. If you poffefs the effential and perdurable privileges of men, how eafily may you difpenfe with the things that have more outward fhew than interior worth, and of which a few years circumfcribe the poffeffion! Honour therefore them, who, by an effect of the diverfity of ftation eftablifhed by Providence, are entitled to honour. Be obedient to them who have a right to command you : but both honour and obey, in a manner confiftent with the excellency of your nature, generoufly and nobly, not with meannefs and abject fervility; and account it no misfortune that you have no fhare in that fupremacy and honour. Seek only to embellifh your fpirit with knowledge and virtue, to maintain your moral freedom, to renew yourfelves after the likenefs of God, and to become fitted for a bleffed immortality; fo, in whatever condition you are, will you be great and happy,

appy, both in the prefent and in the better world.

And you, who have dominion and authority in your hands, you who, by the ftation you fill in human fociety, or by the
other advantages that adorn you, are fo far
exalted above your brethren, never forget
that thofe who are beneath you poffefs
what principally ennobles man, what gives
him his greateft worth, in common with
you; that their nature is as excellent as
yours; that they have the fame deftination
with you; and that they are moftly perifh-
able and tranfitory things by which you
are diftinguifhed from them. Beware, then,
of confidering them in a manner as if they
were beings of an inferior order to you;
and conftantly reflect, that nothing, abfolutely nothing, can make a man mean and
contemptible but folly and vice. Teftify,
much rather, even to the loweft among
mankind, the efteem and affection that is
their

their due as rational and immortal creatures, as children of our univerfal Father
in heaven, as co-heirs of your futurè glory; the regard and love which God and his
fon Jefus have fhewn to them, and everlaft-
ingly will fhew.

And you all, who bear the name of
chriftians, confefs likewife here the excellency of the gift with which God has favoured you in the chriftian doctrine. To
this doctrine you are chiefly indebted for
the knowledge you have of the dignity of
your fpirit, and its high vocation. To this
doctrine you are indebted for knowing the
means whereby you may maintain this dignity of your fpirit, and reach the ends of
its formation. This divine doctrine has
guided us to the way of truth, has removed
the grand impediments that might have
ftopped our progrefs on it, and given us
both light and force to walk with firmer ftep
the courfe appointed us by heaven.

O, Chrif-

O, Chriftians, revere this heavenly doctrine, to which you are fo much indebted.
Beware how you mifufe this gracious prefent, or apply it only to the adorning of
your minds. Let the light, with which it
enlightens you, ftrike' into your hearts, fo
as to chear and fertilize them to noble difpofitions. Let it not only guide you in
difcerning and judging, but let it direct
your inclinations and regulate your conduct. Think and act, at all times, fo as
becomes creatures whofe origin is fo illuftrious, whofe powers are fo great, whofe
ordination is fo glorious. And whenever
temptations flatter, whenever the men of
this world would feduce you to take part
in their follies and exceffes, then let thefe
thoughts be prefent to your mind: What!
fhall I debafe my rational and immortal
foul? Shall I prefer grofs gratifications to
the pure and noble pleafures of the mind?
Shall I, in foolifh and fenfual purfuits,
plunge from the eminence on which I ftand,

as

as the image of the Deity, into the mirey
pool of wallowing beasts? Shall I surren-
der, and difqualify myfelf for, the happinefs to which I am invited in the world to
come, that I may enjoy a few fleeting
goods and fallacious joys of the prefent,
or that I may gratify particular perfons,
and purchafe their favour at the expence
of my innocence and peace? No; I will
endeavour to maintain the poft my Creator
has affigned me, and worthily to employ
the talents he has intrufted to my care,
that he may intruft me, as a faithful fer-
vant, with more hereafter, and requite the
ufe he finds agreeable of my faculties and
advantages with higher advantages and
greater powers. To know him, to converfe with him, to direct my heart and
my life by his will, to ftrengthen in me
each beneficent, each friendly propenfity,
to become conftantly wifer and better, and
even now to purfue a heavenly courfe,
fhall be my chief concern, my glory, and

7   my

my joy. This fhall fupply the want or the lofs of all earthly diftinctions, tranf-port me beyond time and the grave, and lay a firm bafis for my everlafting per-fection and happinefs. And may this be the purpofe and endeavour of us all! may this be our future portion!

ESTI-

ESTIMATE XVIII.

THE

VALUE,

OR

THE IMPORTANCE,

OF THE

DOCTRINE

OF OUR

IMMORTALITY.

If in this life only we have hope in Chrift,
we are of all men moft miferable.

1 Cor. xv. 19.

THE
VALUE,
OR THE
IMPORTANCE,
OF THE
DOCTRINE OF OUR
IMMORTALITY.

QUIET and Satisfaction are the
great objects of our defire; and while
fo much pains are taken to acquire them,
the more is it to be lamented, that we do
not with greater frequency and care make
ufe of that principal fource of true repofe
and fatisfaction, the hope of a bleffed immortality. If you fix your thoughts to
this earth; if you confine your hopes to

R 2   the

the fhort moment of this terreftrial life; if you take this ftate of difcipline and exer- cife for the ultimate fcope of your being ; if you regard barely the prefent, and lofe fight of the future ; then it is no wonder if you perceive diforder, confufion, and mifery on all fides around you ; it is no wonder that you fhould be tormented by doubt and perplexity, that you feek for the true calm and repofe of your fpirit in vain. Only foar above that which is vifible and tranfitory ; do but raife yourfelf in thought to the future world; make yourfelf ac- quainted with the eternity that awaits you; and the greateft part of the difficultics that difturb you will foon vanifh away ; you will perceive the wifeft arrangement, the moft admirable beauty in the conftitution of the world and of your prefent ftate ; you will find ample caufe for contentment in all cir- cumftances, and for bearing all the difficul- ties of this life with firmnefs of mind. The confiderations with which I mean, at
prefent,

present, to furnish your piety, will, I hope
and truft, by the Divine Affiftance, fhed
more light upon the matter.

I fhall fhew you the certain hope of a
bleffed immortality as the principal and
pureft fource of tranquillity and fatisfaction,
and lay before your minds the ineftimable
value of the doctrines and promifes the
gofpel delivers to us, with regard to futurity. And how can I better execute this
defign than by comparing the dark and
melancholy life, and the difmal end of a
man without hope, with the bright and
chearful life and the comfortable end of a
chriftian, who expects a bleffed immortality from a confident belief in the affurances
of the Redeemer! Let us, therefore, fet
thefe two claffes of men againft each other,
and, by attending them through the principal compartments of their lives, we may
perhaps clearly perceive which of them has
the advantage of the other.

To

To the man who knows nothing of futurity, who has no hope of immortality, all nature is a fealed book, and he is the greateft of all myfteries to himfelf. The defign of his exiftence is incomprehenfible to him ; and of the purpofes for which the other creatures that furround him were formed, and which fo far exceed mankind in number, magnitude, and beauty, he knows ftill lefs. Every thing he fees and hears is to him an ænigma, to the folution whereof he can find no key. Reprefent to yourfelf a philofopher, who knows nothing of the gofpel, and from whom futurity is concealed, profoundly contemplating the heaven and the earth, and himfelf, and that you hear him difcourfe on thefe important objects in his comfortlefs folitude : what a doubtful, what a defultory, and difmal language he holds! Methinks I hear him exclaim, in a doleful voice, Why is the heaven fo beautifully adorned, and to what end is this magnificence which nature fo

pro-

profufely difplays wherever I turn my view ?
What is the purpofe of this great, this
immenfe and ingenious ftructure ? How
gloomy, how painful to me is this profpect,
fo charming in itfelf, as I, perhaps now for
the laft time, enjoy it, and at all events
fhall fhortly be deprived of all fentiment
for ever! Were I fhut up in fome dark
and difmal dungeon, had the day never
fhone upon my dwelling, my mifery had
then been tolerable: but here, like fome
malefactor, I fit imprifoned in a gorgeous
palace, but can find nothing delightful,
nothing agreeable in it, as expecting every
moment the fummons to death! — And
what mean the faculties I feel within me?
How am I benefited by the capacities I
poffefs, but which I cannot employ? I behold many beauties, much magnificence,
many aftonifhing effects before me; I am
curious to invefigate and underftand them;
but they are all incomprehenfible to me;
it is too high for me, I cannot reach it.

R 4   My

My faculties forfake me, and the light itfelf is darknefs to me.—It is true, nature
is beautiful; fhe is pleafant and charming;
fhe invites my fenfes to abundance of pleafure and joy. But why, then, am I fo reftlefs and uneafy? Why cannot all thefe
goods and beauties fatisfy my fpirit?
Whence proceeds the want I feel amidft
this abundance, and the fentiment of which
fo often difturbs my livelieft pleafure, and
always renders it incomplete? Why is my
inquifitivenefs never to be fatisfied? Why
do I never ceafe from wifhing? Whence
comes the difguft that fo quickly fucceeds
to enjoyment, and deprives all I earneftly
longed after, in a moment, of its worth?
Has the Creator, then, called me out of
nothing for my torment? Has he given me
fuch defires for the augmentation of my
mifery? To what purpofe fuch great preparatives for the few and uncertain hours
of life?—Thus does the hopelefs mortal
entangle himfelf in reflection. He finds
himfelf

himfelf in the moft delightful garden; but it is all a labyrinth to him, to him it lofes every charm from his want of a clue to guide him through it.

Before the chriftian, who expects immortality, and an eternity of life to come, all these difficulties vanifh away. He fees that it is a wife and benignant God, who has placed him on the globe of the earth. He difcovers the principal fcope of things, and fets his mind at reft. The hope of futurity gives every thing, beautiful and great, he fees in the world, a heightened colour and a new difplay. The view of the boundlefs creation, that utterly perplexed and confounded yonder unhappy being, infpires the chriftian with admiration, and leads him to adore the Moft High in ferenity and fatisfaction. He exclaims, with the author of the Pfalms, " Lord, how glorious are thy works ! in wifdom haft thou made them all ; the earth is full of thy riches !"

Here

Here I perceive everlasting effects: here I find materials for inceffant difcovery; here I feé fources of knowledge and joy, whence rational beings may draw for ever, without any fear of their failing. How gloomy to me would be the contemplation of beautiful nature! how fad the fentiment of my powers! how difficult to affuage my thirft after knowledge! how fertile in vexation my infinite defires! if I had to dread, in a few moments, the utter extinction of knowledge and enjoyment! But thou haft ordained me, O God, to life, to a life that fhall know no end! At prefent my capacities are too great to exhibit themfelves in all their ftrength. The body of death furrounds me, and fixes narrow limits to the workings of my mind. But foon fhall I be free from thefe bonds. My foul will foar aloft, and mount into the realms of light: fhe will rife at the refurrection of the juft, and be liable to defcend no more. Then, O my gracious God, then fhall I firft behold

hold thy works in all their extent, in all
their beauty and fplendour; then fhall I be
for ever employed in the inveftigation of
them, and never be weary of admiring thy
wifdom and power; then will all my defires
be fatisfied, and all my wifhes accom-
plifhed! This is not the place of my final
appointment : it is but preparatory to a far
better and more glorious ftate. Here it is
my bufinefs, by generous occupations, to
begin to qualify myfelf for the purer delights that await me in that world, and
even what I call difficult and imperfect in
my prefent condition muft, if I properly
apply it, promote my future perfection.
Thus does the chriftian underftand the defign of his being, and the tendency of his
powers; and thus does he difpel the darknefs that furrounds him on earth by the
light of the gofpel, which difclofes to his
view the faireft profpects of eternity.

Knowledge

Knowledge and virtue are, indeed, in and for themfelves, and without regard to futurity, the ftrongeft fupports and the richeft fources of our happinefs. How, without knowledge, fhould we fatisfy the curiofity of our minds? How, without virtue, fhould we tranquillize our hearts? How fhould we tame our turbulent paffions, how fhould we controul them when they contend with each other, and bring them to a rational equilibrium, if we were deftitute of knowledge and virtue? Let us only compare the mortal without hope with the chriftian that expects eternity, and fee which of them has the greateft means, and the greateft encouragement, to build his happinefs on this foundation, and to render his life pleafant by knowledge and virtue. We will here allow them both to fpeak their natural fentiments, by which it will plainly appear which of them has the advantage of the other. It is true, knowledge is ornamental to the mind; thus fpeaks the man whofe

hopes

hopes are confined to this life. I experience, that what thinks within me is capable of mounting above vifible objects,
and of piercing into the combination of
things. I feel a great pleafure when I increafe my ideas, and can difcover the traces
of the wife Author of nature. But how,
foolifh and unprofitable is this my employment! Wifdom cannot be acquired without
much toil. Truth never appears to her vo-
taries till after many fuccefslefs refearches!
one may fall into a hundred errors fooner
than difcover one truth. We muft dedi-
cate both day and night to the ftudy of the
hidden operations of nature, before we can
acquire but a flight knowledge of her
fecrets. Mean time, the fpirit grows weary:
its powers diminifh; the body is weakened
by too ftrenuous exertions, and I become
daily lefs capable of tafting the pleafures of
fenfe. And what is, at length, the refult
of all my pains? After a few moments
are paft I fhall be no more, and my labo-
rioufly

riously acquired knowledge will likewise be no more. That which thinks in me, and often foolishly soars above the clouds, will in a few days be loft to exiftence. The great difcoveries I am ftriving to make will vanifh into thin air, and my lofty imaginations, and my exalted conceptions, will be enveloped in the fhades of everlafting night. Such is the language of the man who has no views beyond the grave. His endeavours after knowledge muft necef-farily appear ridiculous to himfelf; and he has little or nothing to encourage him in the profecution of it.

No lefs feeble are his motives to Virtue, and his purpofe to follow her precepts will as eafily fail. She fades like a flower that fprings up on a parched foil, or in a ftoney ground. Virtue, though great her native beauty, is yet not long lived to the man who looks upon death as the period of his being; fhe has not fufficient attractions to
make

make him conftant and true to her love.
Self-intereft and the hope of advantage are
the principal fprings of human actions:
but only few men are fo enlightened as to
fee, at once, the connection between virtue
and felf-love and with real advantage. It
cofts a man labour and toil before he can
arrive at a certain fkill in goodnefs. He
has many obftacles to conquer, and many
difficulties to encounter, if he would fulfill
all his duties with exactitude, and conduct
himfelf in all, circumftances like a true
chriftian. Riches, and honours, and days
of eafe, are not always the companions of
integrity. How often, on the contrary, is
it attended by poverty and fcorn! Nay, is
it any thing uncommon for the brighteft
virtue to be oppofed with animofity, and
perfecuted with vengeance? An yet it is
impoffible, without virtue, to acquire tranquillity of mind, or fatisfaction of heart.
Vice, on the other han!, is often tricked
out with charms: fhe holds out, to her vo-

4   taries,

taries, power and authority, opulence and veneration ; fhe promifes them the greateft enjoyments. And yet Vice renders us un-happy, and, fo long as we are flaves to her, it is impoffible for us to be calm and con-tented. Therefore, if man is to flee from vice, and be in love with virtue ; if he is thereby to live contented and happy; then he muft have certain impelling motives thereto. But do you imagine that any one, who has no penalty to fear in futurity, and no reward to expect, is in a capacity to vanquifh all temptations to evil, and to devote himfelf to the fervice of infulted Virtue and unnoticed Integrity ? Certainly not. Her beauty might probably attract him ; he might even determine to follow her precepts : but how long would his re-folution laft ? The firft violent temptation would put it out of his mind. Were he frankly to explain himfelf, it is thus he would fpeak : What will it profit me, if I earneftly ftrive to be virtuous ? What avails

this

3

this unremitted attention to all my thoughts, my defires, and actions? thefe violent con- flicts with my propenfities and paffions? How difficult it is to conquer onefelf! And what advantage, what fruit, have I at laft to expect from the victory? My pro- bity will be taken for felfifhnefs, my piety will pafs only for fadnefs of heart, and I fhall fit folitary in the duft; while others, of laxer principles, are lolling in the feats of honour! What have I to provide for but my body and my temporal affairs? Why fhould I quarrel with the charms and delights that fo many others enjoy? Shall I embitter my life by the reftrictions of temperance, and for the fake of a fanciful fpiritual pleafure, deny myfelf the more fure and fubftantial pleafures of fenfe? I have nothing to fear, or to hope, after death! So fpeaks the hopelefs mortal: thus will his purpofes to follow virtue be enfeebled: thus he allows himfelf to be feduced by the wages of fin; and difcontent and vexation, perplexity and fear, and every difaftrous' confequence of vice, at once take poffeffion of his heart. From want of hope, he neglects the principal and pureft fources of earthly happinefs, and will always be becoming more un-happy than he was.

Quite otherwife is it with the chriftian, who expects immortality : he daily endeavours to augment his knowledge, and to improve in virtue, and thus daily promotes his true felicity. He can never be wanting in encouragement to his noble endeavours, never in firmnefs and zeal; and the futurity which is ever in his view, renders all he undertakes, in this defign, not only eafy but pleafant. How pleafant, he fays in the fimplicity of his heart, how pleafant to me are the meditations I indulge on the perfections of my God and Father, the greateft and beft of beings ! What a pure delight ftreams through my foul, when I confider

his

2

his ways and admire his works! How it exalts my fpirits when I perceive the wifdom of the Creator in his creatures, and find out the marks of his greatnefs! How my foul repofes in my Divine Redeemer, and in the commiffion he fulfilled on earth! My knowledge indeed, in all refpects, is but imperfect and weak; but this fhall not difhearten me from conftantly labouring, with renewed ardour, at its extenfion and improvement. In the matters of moft importance I have the gofpel for my guide, and am fafe from all deception : by that I perceive an eternity approaching. The real knowledge I fhall here collect, is out of the power of that fpoiler, death. Hereafter, in the empire of fpirits, I fhall purfue my refearches; what is falfe will evaporate from my attainments; and what is folid and juft will form the bafis of my higher perfection. Thus does the hope of futurity excite the chriftian; and the pleafure he procures from his meditations on

reli-

religion and nature will be ever increasing, as he has no need to fear it will ever be loft.

The fame influence, likewife, has hope upon his virtue, as the other fource of human happinefs. It renders him inflexible againft every temptation to wrong; and he renounces all things with joy, fo foon as he thinks on the future world. How eafy, how blefled, he exclaims, is the fervice of my God! and how gracious is the Lord whom I ferve, as fo richly to requite my feeble endeavours in goodnefs, as to reward them for ever! No, my honeft applications to pleafe him are not in vain. Godlinefs has the promifes of this life, and of that which is to come. The Lord commands me to believe that he is the rewarder of them that feek him. Coft what it will to gain the victory over myfelf, yet how glorious are the triumphs I fhall obtain! Virtue, even at prefent, affords me the fincereft

cereft pleafure, and of this pleafure it is not in death to defpoil me ; it will for ever continue, and for ever increafe. And fhall I allow myfelf to be turned afide from the path of rectitude, and make fhipwreck of my future happinefs, for riches, for earthly honours, for fenfual gratifications, for fugacious trifles ? No ; rather forgetting thofe things which are behind, and reaching forth unto thofe things which are before, I prefs toward the mark, for the prize of the high calling of God in Chrift Jefus. Such are the reflections of the chriftian, in expectation of a blelfed immortality. Though knowledge and virtue be a grievous burden to him who is deftitute of hope, yet are they the fources of the moft refined and exalted joys to the man that is fure of eternal life.

To proceed in our comparifon of the hopelefs mortal with the perfuaded chriftian, let us, thirdly, contraft their difpofi-

tions

tions and comportment together. How hard misfortunes bear on him who knows no other and no better life than this! So long as riches, and honours, and worldly joys, fall copioufly to his fhare, he may find the means of concealing his wretchednefs and his deplorable condition from himfelf. The dazzling glare of terreftrial happinefs may offufcate his mind, and hinder him from ftedfaftly fixing his eyes within, and from feeling acutely the deficiency of hope. But, is he vexed with adverfity and forrow, the glittering charms of honour and refpect that furround him vanifh away: the rapturous frenzy, that for fome moments prevented him from viewing his deplorable ftate, is come to an end: he is now thrown back upon himfelf. He now fees clearly the emptinefs and vanity of all that is vifible and terrene: he experiences how infufficient the poffeffion and enjoyment of them are to the contentment of his infinite defires. Where will he now find reft!

Where

Where will he feek comfort and pleafure !
While he is in ignorance of the comfort
. which religion and the hope of immortality
afford us, it is impoffible for him to be at
peace. All his ground of confolation confifts in thefe fad ideas : it is thus with me ;
and all my lamentations cannot alter my
fate. And what now will be the effect of
thefe ideas ? Will the afflictions he fuffers
be thus rendered more tolerable ! Will this
caufe them to abandon the attack? Will
he learn to confider and ufe them as means
to a fuperior kind of happinefs ? No ; if
they be great, then they fink him into a certain infenfibility, into a ftate alike devoid
of pleafure and of pain ; and even this infenfibility is very apt to be deftroyed by
intenfe and keen reflection, and to be fuc-
ceeded by the moft cruel anguifh of mind.
The mortal, who has nothing to hope for
beyond the grave, thus has the full weight
of misfortune to bear, without the poffibi-
lity of tolerably fupporting himfelf under
S 4 it.

it. If he lofe his outward advantages, or
poffeffions, he lofes his all; he knows of
nothing that can repair his damage. The
fources of his happinefs are ftopped; how
then can the enjoyment of them continue?
If he lofe his friends, he lofes them, in his
opinion, for ever: his lofs is irreparable;
and it is not to be wondered at, if an in-
curable forrow takes poffeffion of his foul,
and he gives himfelf up to defpair.

Confider, on the other hand, the chriftian in misfortune, and fee how patient,
how firm, and how chearful, the hope of
futurity makes him! Indeed, he likewife
feels afflictions when they come upon him,
and they frequently force the tears from
his eyes: he tenderly bemoans the lofs of
his friend; it hurts him when he is unjuftly
deprived of his honour, and he is obliged
to undergo the bitter effects of contempt:
it affects him when he is defpoiled of his
goods, and is thereby deprived of the
means

means of generoufly affording relief, and
the exalted delight it occafions: it gives
him concern when he is prevented, by bodily infirmities or pains, to be of fervice to
his neighbour, and of ufe to the world; it
cuts him to the quick when he fees virtue
defpifed, and the nobleft actions go unre-
warded, or indeed repaid with injuries. In
the mean time, however, he does not ceafe
to be happy. He has learned how to moderate his forrows from the doctrines of
religion, and to procure himfelf comfort
in the greateft misfortunes. Is he fcorned
and perfecuted for his godlinefs and piety;
he rejoices in this, that he fuffers with
Chrift, as he knows that he fhall alfo reign
with him hereafter, and that the light afflictions of this prefent time are not to be
compared with the glory he is then to enjoy. Does he lofe his temporal poffeffions;
he is affured, that no man can take from
him the teftimony of a good confcience,
the pleafure of virtue, and the grace of his
God,

God. He defpifes the advantages and treafures of the world, and fixes his view on
the great reward the righteous judge fhall
give him at that day. And fhould the in-
juſtice of mankind compel him to abandon
his country, and to wander, a vagabond, in
mifery on the earth, even this likewife he
has learned how to bear. He looks up to
a city whofe builder and maker is God; he
difregards whatever is vifible, and directs
his attention to the things that are not feen,
and his converfe is in heaven. Are his
friends taken from him by remorfelefs
death, or does fome fecret difpenfation re-
move him far from fuch as his foul holds
dear; the expectation of futurity can even
mitigate thefe bittereſt of forrows. No
diftance, no feparation, no death, can part
him for ever from the friend of his heart.
He will find him again in the kingdom of
the juſt : he will there renew the bonds of
amity with him, and, in that glorious ftate,
nothing can difturb their noble and virtuous
friend-

friendſhip. Thus the hope of the chriſtian can never be put to confuſion. It alleviates to him each attack of calamity, which
bears the hopeleſs down to the ground, and
plunges him in utter deſpair.

Let us, laſtly, caſt an eye on theſe two
perſons, while lying on the bed of death,
and conſider their different exits from the
world. Approach the unhappy man who
feels himſelf dying, and yet is totally deſti-
tute of all hope of another and better life !
fee how anxiety and diſmay diſtort his
viſage ! how he wrings his hands from perturbation and diſtreſs ! what gloomy looks
he caſts on the perſons around him ! Death
appears to him in his moſt dreadful form !
he is truly the king of terrors ! and, poor
man, he has nothing that he can uſe as a
covering againſt his darts, nothing to which
he can addreſs himſelf for comfort in this
moſt awful moment ! He ſees himſelf turn-
ing to duſt, he ſees the grave and corruption

tion before him, and cannot call up a hope
that he fhall ever be ranfomed. The
thought of his annihilation ftrikes a chill-
nefs through his foul, and fills it with infurmountable terrors. Whatever has hitherto brought him pleafure and joy, is now
flown from his imagination, and is departed
for ever. He now, for the laft time, fees
the orb of day, the all-reviving fun, and
is in expectation of an eternal night. His
friends take leave of him for ever, and
their charming converfe, as he thinks, will
never chear him again. He muft quit all
things without any hope of acquiring more!
—Can you figure to yourfelves a more deplorable condition than this?

On the other hand, obferve the chrif-
tian, who, confiding in the promifes of our
Saviour, looks for a bleffed immortality!
How inftructive are his laft moments, and
how calmly he meets death and eternity!
Death is to him a meffenger of peace; he

announces

announces deliverance and freedom; he conducts him to life, to a far better and completer life than the prefent. Why fhould he not willingly follow his call? Why fhould he not readily exchange this life for the other? He lofes nothing that will not be reftored to him, or be infinitely over-balanced. He has already a prefentiment of the joys that await him; and, the nearer his end approaches, his countenance brightens, and his foul is more cheared. He haftens to the place of his deftination with a pious impatience, and may addrefs his forrowing friends with comfortable affurance : " Weep not for me, O my friends, I fhall foon embrace you in another life; continue to truft in your great Redeemer !" Thus dies the chriftian, full of hope, and enters into the joy of his Lord.

This is the vaft difference between the hopelefs mortal, and the chriftian that looks for a bleffed eternity. Thefe are the in-comparable

comparable privileges the one poffeffes more than the other. To the former all nature is an unfathomable myftery, and the purport of his own exiftence is out of his fight: the latter knows to what he is ordained, and the creation is to him the mirror of the perfections of its Author. Knowledge and virtue, the fources of our happinefs, are fhut againft the one, and he has little or nothing to induce him to apply to them for repofe: to the other, to the chriftian, thefe fources of pleafure ftand conftantly open; and in the knowledge of truth, and the practice of virtue, he finds the moft permanent joy. The former finks under the weight of misfortune: the latter rejoices in tribulations, and no accident can rob him of his happinefs. The former lofes all courage in death, and fhudders at the approach of his end: the latter, the juft man, has even hope in his death, and firft begins properly to live, when he feems to be dying. Muft you not confefs,

confefs, then, that, as chriftians, we poffefs
infinitely greater advantages than the man
who does not believe in the promifes of
the gofpel? Muft we not allow, that we
fhould be the moft miferable of all creatures, if our hopes were bounded by the
limits of this life, if, after it, we had no
other, no better to expect? How many
caufes, therefore, have we to praife and
commemorate the benignity of our Saviour,
who has brought life and undecaying exiftence to light by the gofpel? How can we
be grateful enough to him for the victory
he has enabled us to obtain over death and
the grave! for the glorious views he has
given us of futurity! Does not fuch a
Teacher, does not fuch a Benefactor, merit
all our veneration? Does he not merit the
utmoft devotion of our heart, our moft
willing obedience? What low difpofitions
fhall we not betray, if we defpife the gofpel
of the Son of God, if we think flightly of
his promifes, and reject the felicity to which
we

we are called? No, we will not do so; we have the happiness of being christians; we have the hope of everlasting life. Let us prize this happiness as it deserves; let us walk worthy of this hope. Let us break forth in shouts of triumph to our glorified Redeemer, who has delivered us from the dread of annihilation, and given us the assurance of everlasting life. But let us also shew, by our whole deportment, what mighty expectations we have. How ill would it become us, christians, to seek our rest, our satisfaction, our happiness, in the things of the earth, since we are devoted to eternity! How ill would it become us, to be inconsoleable at the loss of our earthly goods, or of our dearest friends, like the heathens who are destitute of hope! How irrationally should we act, if we should only provide for our body, and bestow no regard on the soul! How bitterly shall we hereafter lament our foolish choice, if we prefer the hard bondage of vice to the easy fervice of virtue, and fo lofe the refined delights and the eternal felicities of heaven! Oh, then, animate yourfelves to a generous and holy conduct, ye chriftians, created and redeemed to an immarceffible glory! Set loofe your hearts from every thing fuga-cious and earthly. Never fix your defires and views to the objects on this fide the grave. Raife yourfelves often in thought to eternity; endeavour to excite and confirm in yourfelves a heavenly mind, and let your whole behaviour be regulated by the future world. Evince in all things, even in the moft deplorable events of life, that you are chrif-tians, who look not fo much on the things that are feen, as on thofe that are not feen. Do honour to the religion you profefs by a fteady and chearful virtue, and take faft hold on the hope that Chrift has given you. It will not fail you, even in death; and you will enter, rejoicing, into the kingdom of your God.

Eafter-Day.

ESTIMATE XIX.

THE

VALUE

OF

MAN's LIFE-TIME

UPON

EARTH.

Man is like a thing of nought: his time paffeth
away like a fhadow.   Pfalm cxliv. 4.

THE

VALUE

OF

MAN's LIFE-TIME

UPON

EARTH.

NOTHING is by many perſons more thoughtleſsly laviſhed away than their time. They hold nothing to be more inſignificant than an hour, a day, or a week. Therefore, as they have always time enough for every thing, they drive every thing off from one time to another, and take no account of its loſs. Therefore it is that time ſeems, by their feelings, ſo tedious in its progreſs, hangs often heavy on their hands, and makes them anxiouſly long for each

ſuc-

fucceffive change or fection of it. Therefore it is, that they are fo feduloufly atten-
tive to the means of fhortening their time,
and fo eager to feize on any thing that promifes them this favour. Therefore, every
diffipation, every company, every amufe-
ment, every greater or leffer public fpec-
tacle, be it never fo terrifying or alarming,
finds fo hearty a welcome.—Would one not
imagine that perfons who think in this manner were fure of their lives for hundreds or
thoufands of years to come, and that the
profpect of this long continuance filled
them with perturbation and horror? And
yet thefe are beings of yefterday, and will
probably fee nothing of to-morrow! Men,
whofe time flits away like a fhadow! Men,
whofe longeft life is as fhort as it is uncertain, and who even themfelves but too frequently complain of the brevity and uncertainty of it! Whence, then, this direct contradiction to themfelves? How can one
and the fame fubject have fuch oppofite
quali-

qualities, and occafion fuch oppofite judgements? Becaufe it is not always feen in the
fame point of view, not always enjoyed by
the fame meafure and rule; becaufe it is
not always judged of by what in and of itfelf it is, but according to the prefent fentiments a man has of it, and the ufe to
which he applies it. Is the time ftill future,
do whole months and years lie ftill between;
then its tedious approach makes the man
of the world impatient: is it prefent, and
he knows not well how to employ it; then
the weight of it is a burden: is it paft, has
it flipped from him unufed and unenjoyed;
then he laments the fhortnefs and velocity
of it: mere miftakes; which he alone
avoids, who knows how to eftimate the
value of time, and conftantly to make a
good ufe thereof. To him the time that is
allotted him on earth is of the utmoft importance, as he underftands its deftination
and employment, and in the application of
it has both of them conftantly in view.

T 4

The

The time of our life upon earth is important, it is of great value, as it is short, and of uncertain duration. He need not be very choice of his time, and might be somewhat prodigal of it, who had some thousands of years to live, and was sure of his life! But by no means he who can scarcely count so many days, and cannot reckon upon one with any assurance! Yes, short is the longest life of man, and very few of the species attain to the utmost limits of it. Numbers are obliged to quit the course, while yet they have scarce entered upon it; have hardly advanced a few steps, ere they know any thing either of its tendency, or its pleasures, or its sorrows. And how many others are snatched away by death, before they have left the half of it behind, and come at once to the goal they thought such a distance off! And what are even seventy or eighty years to such as have passed them? Are they any thing more than a transient morning's dream to a being that

looks

looks for immortality, and feels inexhauftible powers and infatiable defires within
him ? And who of us all can tell whether
he fhall dream out this dream, or whether
he fhall not much fooner wake in another
fcene of things ? Who of us knows whether the prefent year may not be the laft,
whether the prefent day may not be the laft
to him ? As certainly as we are all here at
prefent alive, fo certainly will more than
one of us be no longer on the earth by the
end of this year. And this may be the
portion of the youngeft, the healthieft, the
ftrongeft, as well as the aged and infirm;
it may attack any one of us, however great
the fenfation of his vital powers may be at
prefent ! And muft not the time, which is
fo fhort and uncertain, be of great value to
us ? Can we afford to fquander any of it
away ? Can we allow any of it to run to
wafte ? Did the youth know, that, even in
the fpring-tide of his life, he may become
a prey to death ; that he may bloffom here,

but

but not bear fruit; did the man reflect that
he may not reach the pinnacle of extreme
old age; that he may be thrown into the
grave in the midſt of his courſe; how very
differently would both the one and the other
apply and enjoy their appointed time!
how carefully would the former cheriſh and
guard, in the bloom of his life, the innocence that is to be the ground of his bliſs
in a better world! and how zealouſly would
the other ſtrive to anſwer his vocation!
But does either the one or the other know
the contrary of this, with any aſſurance?
Can the former reckon, with certainty, on
ſeeing the ſummer? can the latter, on ſeeing
the autumn of his life? And ſhould not
both of them, then, ſo uſe the few uncertain years they have to live, as though
every one of them were the laſt?

The time of our life on earth is, farther,
very important, it is of great value, as it
fleeth away with incredible ſpeed. Place
thyſelf

thyſelf upon the margin of the rapid torrent; obſerve with what inceſſant force one
drop purſues another, one wave drives on
another, how every moment the ſurface of
the ſtream is changed, how ſoon and how
far what thou faweſt but now is rolled away
beyond the ſight, and how it flows together
to the larger river, and then, with the river
itſelf, is abſorbed in the ocean; then wilt
thou have a ſimilitude of the velocity with
which thy hours, thy days, thy years, flow
away. Yes, every thing, as it were, adds
fleetneſs to time ! What a conſiderable portion of it are we robbed of by ſleep, the
brother of death ! How cloſe together,
how blended, are commonly the moment
of being awake and the firſt inſtant of ſleep !
How imperceptible, how totally effaced
from our remembrance, how completely
annihilated is the ſeparation between them !
And then the various and ſucceſſive affairs
of life, which admit of no delay, conſtantly
purſuing and driving each other on ; the

daily,

daily, the hourly revolutions and changes
of every thing about us; our own reftlefs
endeavours after fome end, after greater
activity and happinefs, after new pleafures
and profpects; the multitude and variety
of views, of projects, of concerns, of expectations, of obftacles, of impulfes, of
joys and forrows, which are continually
meeting, purfuing, overtaking, or impeding
us in the path of life; how much muft
thefe accelerate the race of time! Yes,
rapid, inconceivably rapid, is its current!
Ere we have looked about us, it is gone;
ere we have made up our minds, the opportunity for doing or enjoying good is
paft. Nothing can detain its flight, nothing
abate the rapidity of its courfe. Tirefome
as it may frequently feem, in regard to our
wifhes and expectations, fo quickly is it
elapfed when once it is arrived; and he
who knows not how to prize its worth, and
does not feel its value, he who does not
account of hours and moments as well as

of

of days and years, to him will the greater part of it flow on unufed and unenjoyed.

The time of our life on earth is of confequence: thirdly, it is of great value, as it is irrevocable. Once paft, it is gone for ever. Once elapfed, unufed and unenjoyed, it is for ever loft. No remorfe, no tears, no lamentations, can recall it from the gulph of the paft. Where is the year we finifh to-day? where is the hour we complete this moment? Can we live or enjoy either the one or the other again? O, young man, where is the period of thy guiltlefs childhood? Where are the days of thy blooming youth, O thou that art arrived at manhood? Where is the whole of thy life-time, thy childifh, thy youthful, thy manly, thy advanced age, O thou that art full of years, who trembleft on the brink of the grave? Is not the childhood of the youth, the youth of the man, the whole life-time of the aged, for ever elapfed, irrevocably

vocably elapfed and gone? Which of them all can fet out upon his courfe afrefh, or only tread one pace of it again? Thou wifheft in vain, O thou who haft trifled and fquandered away thy youth, or fpent thy beft years in the fervice of folly and vice, in vain doft thou wifh their return; in vain doft thou repine at the inconceivable velocity with which they efcaped thee; in vain doft thou deplore thy levity, thy heedleffnefs, and the mifufe thou haft made of the faireft feafon, the beft years of thy life! Their lofs is irrecoverable; the ceafelefs torrent of time has carried them away, and nothing can repair the damage thou haft thus brought on thyfelf. The time that is ftill before thee, thou mayft more wifely and better employ, and thereby become happier; but the hours, the days, the years, that are once behind thee, are no more in thy power, and the detrimental effects of the unemployment or abufe of them can never be wholly removed. And muft not the

the time that is fo irrevocable, the lofs of which is fo irreparable, be of great importance and of great value in our eyes? We fhould, furely, be as cautious and provident as poffible in the management of what we may fo eafily neglect and lofe, but which cannot with impunity be neglected and loft.

The time of our life on earth is, fourthly, important; it has a great value, as it is granted us for the purpofe of executing a number of weighty and difficult matters. Oh, how much have we all to do in this fhort fpace of life, if we applied it to the ends for which it is given, if we would be and become here what we are called to be and to become! To fatisfy our animal wants, to procure us food and raiment, to fupport our terreftrial life, to purfue fome art or trade; to provide for the maintenance of our family, to promote the public welfare, and to perform a certain part therein; this

this is not all, this is not the chief of what we have here to perform and bring to effect! To thefe purpofes we have no need of all the great capacities and powers we have received of the Creator, of all the means to higher perfection and happinefs of which he has made us fufceptible! No; here we are to become rational, wife, and virtuous creatures; here we are to get the better of our animal propenfities, to govern ourfelves, to think and live by principles; here we are to love God and our brethren, to direct all our inclinations and defires to the beft and worthieft objects, to feek our fatisfaction in juftice and beneficence, to re-fine and ennoble our tafte, to ftudy to employ all our capacities and powers in the beft manner, and by thefe means to prepare ourfelves for the employments and plea-fures of a higher life. And are thefe, truly, things that are fo quickly, fo eafily effected? Is this, truly, the work of a few hours or days? Do they not require many and reite-

rated

rated attempts, continued practice, inceffant application? Have we not many both
inward and outward impediments and difficulties to encounter by the way?—Can we
ever, in all thefe particulars, become fo
expert, fo complete, that we cannot ftill
become more apt and more perfect? Are
we not capable of a conftantly progreffive,
of an unbounded perfection? And muft
not the time in which we have all this to
do, and which is fo fhort and uncertain, be
important, be precious in our fight? Certainly the man who degrades himfelf, in
his thoughts, to a level with the beafts of
the field, and expects after death to fhare
their lot, may confider the time of his life
on earth as infignificant, and be indifferent
to the ufe of it! But to him who reflects
on his true appointment, who underftands
the dignity of the man and the chriftian,
who confiders and feels his immortality, his
affinity with fuperior beings, and with the
Deity himfelf, to him every day, every

Vol. II.   U   hour

hour of his earthly exiftence, muft and will be highly important. To turn it to the beft account muft and will be, at once, both his duty and his joy.

A fifth circumftance, which renders the time of our life on earth of much importance, and gives it a great value, is this: fhort and uncertain and irrevocable as time is, yet, in every greater or fmaller fection of it, we may do much good or much evil, may be very ferviceable or very hurtful. To this neither a whole ftage of a man's life, nor whole years, nor months, are requifite. Every day may occafion, to ourfelves and others, whole centuries of happinefs or mifery. Every hour may be the parent of a thoufand and a thoufand gloomy or pleafant, chearful or forrowful, hours and days. They all are concatenated together, are all interwoven with each other, and all fruitful in great and important effects. Haft thou lavifhed away and mif-employed

5

one hour, one day, one month, one year of
thy life; thou haft not only loft this time,
and loft it for ever, but its lofs and its
mifufe has the moft baneful influence of
all thy future hours and days, and months
and years. On the other hand, haft thou
well employed the prefent time, whether
long or fhort; haft thou fown good feed
therein, and exercifed thyfelf in ufeful
matters; then wilt thou reap an increafe of
a thoufand fold in the times to come. And
how much good, or how much evil, how
many generally ufeful or generally prejudicial things may we think, and will, and
fpeak, and defign, and do, in one fingle
day, in one fingle hour! How often is a
day, or an hour, a fource of never-failing
joy, or of unremitting forrow, to ourfelves
and others! How often is the foundation
laid of a thoufand agreeable or difagreeable
fenfations, of a thoufand laudable or fhameful actions! How often does a day, or an
hour, tranquillize or difturb, embitter or

U 2 fweeten

sweeten the whole succeeding life! How
often does it strengthen the infirm, or render him weaker still! instruct or confuse
the ignorant! guide the innocent aright,
or seduce him astray! comfort the sufferer,
or multiply his sorrows! amend the wicked,
or corrupt him more! rejoice or grieve the
good! How much is frequently effected by
one thought, one word, one opinion, one
action, one mistake, or one omission! and
how far do its effects extend! And if an
hour or a day may be so important to our-
solves and to others, how important must
whole months, whole years, how important must our whole life-time be! What
a heavy burden of bad, of criminal attempts and actions, must the vicious be
heaping upon themselves during the whole
course of it! And how rich a treasure of
good and divine sentiments and actions, of
actions that God will requite, may the virtuous be collecting together! And must
not the time, wherein we may do this or
the

the other, and one of which we fhall certainly do, be of the greateſt importauce to us?

Yes; the time of our life on earth is important: it is of a great value; for the uſe or neglect of it has an influence on all our future fortunes; their confequences accompany us into the grave, and out of the grave again into the regions of eternity. The prefent, O my chriſtian brother, is the feed-time. If thou doſt not carefully cultivate the field intruſted to thee, if thou doſt not fow good feed therein, or foweſt it fparingly, and doſt not guard and tend it as it fprings up and fills; then thou canſt not hope to reap when the feafon comes; the crop will fail thee; thou wilt fuffer indigence and mifery, or thou wilt reap but fparingly; thou wilt be reduced to eat the bitter and corrupted fruit of thy wicked works. This is the time of exercife and difcipline. Here thou art to allow thyfelf

to be educated, formed, and improved;
here thou art to employ thy faculties and
powers, to exert them as becomes a rational, an immortal creature; to love and to
prize truth and virtue above all things, to
rejoice in God, to obey him chearfully, and
to ftudy contentment and happinefs in the
fulfilling of his will. Doft thou not make
this thy ftudy, rejecteft thou the difcipline
and the inftruction of thy Father in heaven;
doft thou refufe to exercife thyfelf in what
is right and good: then wilt thou proceed,
ignorant, unimproved, and unexpert, from
the fchool of this life, into thy fuperior
appointment: then, at the time of retribu-
tion, thou haft nothing in return for thy
induftry and fidelity to expect; then muft
thou fuffer the penalty due to thy untract-
ablenefs and thy difobedience; then muft
thou, if thou wouldft even there be happy,
then muft thou become fo by much harder,
much feverer difcipline. Here is the time
for preparation: here muft thou learn to
love,

love, and to ufe, and to enjoy, at leaft as
a noviciate, the occupations, the pleafures,
the advantages of the future life, and give
a nobler direction to thy defires and thy
tafte, as is fitting for that fuperior ftate.
Art thou averfe to this; doft thou perfift in
retaining thy animal, thy earthly difpofitions: then muft thy delights, thy pleafures, thy happinefs, finally terminate with
the prefent life; then art thou not fufceptible of the purer delights, the nobler pleafures, the exalted blifs, which, at the time
of enjoyment, await them who have prepared and fitted themfelves for them. But,
well for them, eternally well, who have
actually done fo, and continue to do it!
They may promife themfelves the richeft
harveft from what they have fown, the moft
glorious fruits from the docility with which
they have allowed themfelves to be educated, and the moft blifsful enjoyment from
their careful preparation. And muft not
the time, which thus determines all our fu-

U 4   ture

ture condition, which procures us either blessedness or misery, reward or punish-ment, in the other world; must not this time be important, must it not be of in-estimable value to us?

But if, then, the time of our life on earth be so short and uncertain, if it flit so quickly away, if it be so irrevocable, if it be allotted for the performance of so many weighty and difficult matters; if we may, in every, even in the smallest section of it, do so much good or so much evil, so many generally useful or generally hurtful actions, and if the application of it have so great an influence on our future condition, Oh, then, consider and use this time agreeably to its value, and the purposes for which it is granted! It may be husbanded, but it may likewise be lavished away: it may be comparatively prolonged, but it may like-wise be shortened: it may leave vestiges of its passage behind, which may gladden our-

ourselves and others for ever; it may likewise be totally loft to us and to them. The
former is the aim and the happinefs of the
wife; this the behaviour and the punifhment of fools. O, let that be your aim,
your moft zealous, your inceffant aim!
Treafure the time, the fhort, the uncertain,
the fleeting, the irremeable, the important
time you have here to live; prize each year
of it, each day, every hour. Be not prodigal, be œconomical of your time, of
which you may have fo little left, and of
the application whereof you muft one day
give an account. Let not your time pafs
unemployed, unfertilized away. Let it not
elapfe in idlenefs or vice. Beware of trifling
or fquandering away the hours, the days,
that are fo great and important in their
value, and irreparable in their lofs. Seize
and fructify every moment that is ftill in
your power; mark it with fome reflection,
with fome action not unworthy of a man;
and thereby give a certain fixture and duration

tion. to what is so fleeting and vain. Meditate and effect as much good as you always can; and though you cannot thus stop the rapid progress of time, yet make it memorable to you, and the recollection of it a foundation of joy.—Procrastinate nothing; since the time is uncertain, it is not in your power. Do and enjoy the good to-day, which to-day you are allowed to do and to enjoy; since you know not whether you will have time, and ability, and opportunity, for it to-morrow. Consider, judge, and act, at present, as the present is connected with the future. Frequently reflect, that shortly time will be no more to you; no time for practice and preparation: and the more you have still to do, in regard of your improvement, hasten so much the more to finish this important task.. The farther the day of your earthly life is already spent, so much the more sedulously apply every remaining hour or moment of it to the performance of what you have to do, that
you

you may not be unprepared when the night comes on wherein no man can work. And then, but only then, let your time pafs away like a fhadow! It is not loft; it has been that to you which it was appointed to be, what it was defigned to procure you; and to time, well employed, enfues eternity, wherein we fhall not lament the right ufe of it, wherein we fhall inceffantly enjoy it!

Long and bleffed be your days, my deareft companions and hearers! May chearful confidence and pious joy be their conftant attendants; may hope and reliance on God, and the profpect of a better life, fhed light and happinefs around them! Heightened by wifdom and virtue, may they ferenely glide away; free from all felf-accufing forrows, free from reproaching and anxious cares! May no day of your lives pafs by unufed and unenjoyed; may none of them caufe you perplexity and

and fhame in the folemn hour of death!
None witnefs againft you at the day of
judgement! But may each of them be
marked by ufeful employments, by fome
laudable action, by thankful enjoyment of
the bounties of heaven, each be fruitful in
bleffed effects for the future life! Yes;
though fhort and fleeting your days on
earth, yet may they be rich in the bleffings
of God, in the works of righteoufnefs, in
the works of beneficence and love, and
the memorial of them be as joyful to yourfelves as to your contemporaries, your
children, and your defcendants! And when,
at length, the laft of the days of your life
fhall appear, when you are fummoned to
exchange time for eternity, then may the
peace of God confole and gladden your
hearts, then may you take up the words of
the triumphant apoftle: "I have fought
the good fight; I have finifhed my courfe.
Henceforth there is laid up for me a crown
of righteoufnefs, which the Lord, the righteous

teous Judge, fhall give me!" I have ftood
firm to God and to virtue, and fhall receive the prize from my Judge and my
Father!—Yes; teach us, O God, O our
merciful Father! fo teach us to think, and
to live, that we may pafs through the
grave, and gate of death, into the blifs of
the better, the eternal life!

ESTIMATE XX.

OF

SPIRITUAL

EXPERIENCES.

If any man will do his will, he shall know of
the doctrine, whether it be of God, or whether I speak of myself.   John vii. 17.

O F

THERE are three ways of arriving at the knowledge of truth and certainty; reafon, faith, and experience. Reafon lays before the inquirer certain general prepofitions, received of all men, and fimply irrefragable. She connects and compares known truths together, and, by juft confequences, produces a conclufion, which was either not at all, or not clearly enough, known before. She traces things up to their firft principles, and thereby enlightens and explains them.——Faith refts itfelf on the teftimony of another : it examines the accounts that are given of any matter, and the credibility of the witneffes that deliver them. It compares the different parts of the hiftory together, and with the circumftances wherein they were performed, or happened; and when it finds a fufficient capacity and integrity in the witneffes, and a correfpondence in their narratives, it yields its acquiefcence thereto.—Experience, in fhort, inftructs us of the things that fall under our knowledge, or by the impreffion and effects they produce on our eyes, our ears, or the other organs of fenfe. She gives us alfo to obferve the inward motions or alterations that happen either in our foul or body, and thereby teaches us to form a judgement both of our natural and our fpiritual or intellectual ftate. Would we, then, render our knowledge as perfect as we may, we muft take all thefe three different ways for knowing the truth, and for being certain of it. And this, not merely in regard of human knowledge, but it is likewife neceffary and indifpenfable in regard of religion.

gion. We muſt endeavour to obtain, not only an hiſtorical, but alſo a rational and experimental knowledge of every truth, as far as its nature, and our ſituation, will allow. The more numerous the evidences we have of any matter, the greater will our certainty of it be, and the more completely ſhall we be ſatisfied about it. There are, indeed, doctrines in religion, which we can only know through faith; and the truth of them, in reſpect of us, depends only on hiſtorical narrative. But others, and thoſe the greateſt number, are of ſuch a nature, that they are likewiſe to be known by means of reaſon and experience; and, in ſuch caſes, we may very advantageouſly blend theſe ſeveral ways for arriving at the truth. Revealed religion is chiefly founded on the narratives and the teſtimony of per-ſons who lived many ages before our times. Theſe perſons relate to us, in their writings, the ſad conſequences produced by ſin, and the wiſe arrangements eſtabliſhed by God

X 2 for

for our reftoration and amendment; they difcover to us the counfels and determinations of the Moft High ; they inform us of the fervice he requires of us, and delivers us the conditions we muft fulfil, if we would partake of his favour, and be happy for ever. Thefe narratives, then, are too important, by far, for us to receive and adopt them, without examining the authority on which they ftand. We muft, therefore, difcufs the characters and the credibility of the narrators on whofe authority they depend, and endeavour to require a certainty of their truth. Thefe are the firft means of arriving at knowledge and certainty ; and the effect will be, the introduction of faith. But our knowledge may be ftill more perfect; it may be brought to a higher degree of evidence and certainty, if we purfue the other way, and confult our reafon. Though reafon might not have difcovered the doctrines of revealed religion by her own penetration, yet may fhe

pro-

pronounce upon them after their promul-
gation. She may deduce many of them
from the firſt principles of human knowledge. She may ſhe v us their various and
exact connection with other truths already
known. She may reconcile the ſeeming
contradictions between them. She may
preſent us with new evidence for their
truth. In ſhort, ſhe may draw many neceſſary and important conſequences from
them. Her concurrence makes theſe doctrines the more acceptable, and our certainty of them muſt be ſo much the greater.
But here we are not to ſtop : we muſt likewiſe, in regard of religion, take the way
of experience ; we muſt endeavour to become certain of its truth and excellency
by our own ſenſations. On this experimental knowledge all religion, indeed, depends ; as nothing can ſupply the want of
it, and as all the other kinds of knowledge, unleſs they are connected with this,
are incapable of rendering us happy. We

muſt,

muſt, however, be extremely cautious on this head, left we deceive ourſelves, and fail on ſuch a path as will be very danger-ous both to ourſelves and others.

That I may warn you of this wrong courſe, I have determined to treat ſome-what circumſtantially of a matter that has ſo great an influence on our tranquillity and happineſs, and to ſet it in as plain a light as the ſhort time allowed to theſe diſcourſes will permit. The words of Jeſus, which I have read to you, preſent us with a fit occaſion for theſe reflections. What can he mean but this: If you ſuffer the doc-trine which I deliver to you, in the name of God, to have its due effect upon you; if you follow my precepts, and reduce them to practice, you will infallibly feel their godly power; you will become better thereby, more tranquil, and more pious; you will perceive, by experience, that my doctrine hath a celeſtial origin; that I am

not

not a mere philofopher, but addrefs you as a meffenger from God. Our Lord intimates, therefore, that a man may acquire an experimental knowledge of the truth of religion, and that it is an excellent means of arriving at the complete affurance thereof.

Let us now inveftigate the nature and quality of thefe fpiritual experiences; and remark the principal rules to be obferved in our judgement of them, for preferving us from the ordinary miftakes thereupon.

The term Spiritual Experience is generally ufed in a very indefinite fenfe, and they who boaft the moft about it have frequently the moft obfcure and erroneous conception of it. They adorn with this expreffion every feeling that is fomewhat ftrong, every extraordinary motion of the blood, without firft examining from whence thefe feelings and emotions proceed. They continually confound the imagination and

expe-

experience together, and often look upon the moſt natural changes in their body and mind as fomething extraordinary and fuper-natural. When they are defired to explain their experiences, or to fhew whence they arife, they evade the queſtion by declaring the whole of the matter to be incompre-henfible. But were they at the pains to inquire a little into their own nature, and inform themfelves fomewhat of the man-ner wherein the foul acts upon the body, and the body upon the foul, then many of the incomprehenfibilities, at which they aſtonifh themfelves and others, would fall to the ground, and they would obtain a complete folution of what they at prefent regard as an inexplicable myſtery. When we fpeak of experiences in common life, we all underſtand what the term implies, and what we mean thereby: we denote nothing elfe by it than that we feel the effects of particular things, and are certain of them. Thus we fay, for example, the

power

power of the fun, the property of the air, the violence of the wind, and the like. That is, we feel the effects that thefe things have upon us, the alterations they produce in our bodies, and we are affured of them. Apply this now to fpiritual experiences, and you will have a plain and juft comprehenfion of them. What are they but the feelings of the good effects religion has upon us, of the happy changes it has produced in our thoughts, our judgements, our inclinations, our actions, and our pleafures? This idea is perfectly plain. It coincides with the nature of our foul; and we need only attentively confider what we call fpiritual experiences, for finding that they are no otherwife to be defcribed. I will explain myfelf farther on this matter. The doctrines of religion have not only an enlightening, but alfo an affecting and a perfuafive power. They not only rectify our underftanding, but they alfo ameliorate our wills. They purify our hearts, they determine our defigns and defires, and move us to good and virtuous refolutions. If, then, they produce in us fuch effects, we fhall have a lively knowledge, or, which is the fame thing, we fhall acquire an experimental knowledge of the power and efficacy of the doctrines of religion. A few examples will fet this matter in the cleareft light. Every devout chriftian confiders the gracious difpofitions of God towards finners; he purfues, with filent attention, the wife and good methods which the Moft High hath ordained for reclaiming and reftoring the human race; he admires the greatnefs of the love difplayed in our behalf: he makes the application of it to himfelf. " Me likewife, unworthy as I am," fays he to himfelf, " me hath God loved; even me; even on me hath he fhed his compaffions!" Thefe thoughts affect him, and fill his heart with the fincereft returns of love to his everlafting Benefactor. He has thereby an ex-

perimental

perimental knowledge ot the force of what
religion teaches us of the love of God.
And how ? He feels the good effects that
declaration has upon him, and will thereby
be moved to pious refolutions. So is it
likewife with the other doctrines of religion. When, therefore, the confideration
of the indecency, the hatefulnefs, and the
fhameful confequences of fin, and the ex-
ceeding great difpleafure God hath towards
it, creates in us an actual abhorrence of all
kinds of vice ; when the confideration of
the beauty and amiablenefs of virtue, the
reafonablenefs and excellency of the law
of God and Chrift, and the great obligations we are under to our Creator and Deliverer, infpires us with a predominant inclination to all good, we then experience
the fanctifying efficacy of thefe doctrines.
When the confideration of the wifdom,
might, and goodnefs of the Moft High,
the difplay of his holy and irreproachable
government, and his fatherly care of the
                                    juft ;

juſt; when reflections on the nature and
end of our preſent ſituation, and its connection with the future eternity, lightens
our calamities, tranquillizes our heart,
makes us firm and courageous in misfortune, and teaches us to truſt in the help
of the Lord; then have we a delightful
experience of the ſtrength of theſe conſo-
lations; we feel the ſolidity of the ſupport
religion affords to mankind in afflictions.
Spiritual experiences, then, are, in general,
nothing more than the conſciouſneſs of the
ſalutary effects which the maxims and
rules of conduct, the emotions and conſo-
lations of religion, produce in us. Theſe
effects, however, ariſe from two different
cauſes: one being the proper and peculiar
force of religion, and the other the particular aſſiſtance of the Spirit of God.

The doctrines of religion have in themſelves a natural power to move, and to
convince all thoſe that embrace them, and

to

to direct their conduct this way or that.
This power they have in common with all
other truths. No fooner have we obtained
a plain, juft, lively, and certain knowledge
of fome important truth, but immediately
it has likewife a ftronger or weaker degree
of influence on our heart, imparting to us
either joy or forrow, hope or fear, pleafure
or difpleafure, and inducing us to make a
proper ufe of the lights we have obtained.
Now, as the doctrines of religion are in
their nature much greater, much more elevated, and important, than all others, as
they ftand in the ftrongeft connection with
our prefent and future happinefs, as they
ground their authority on a revelation
from God, fo muft they neceffarily have a
greater power to act upon the will; and it
is impoffible for us to behold them with a
certain degree of perfpicuity and energy,
and to apply them home, without feeling
that they have an effect upon our defires
and averfions, our inclinations and abhor-
rences,

rences, without being moved to follow the
information we have acquired, and to make
it the rule of our whole deportment.

Since, therefore, what we call fpiritual
experiences are produced no lefs by our
natural faculties than the intrinfic power
of the doctrines of the gofpel, we are not
to wonder that we are often deceived when
we would ftate the peculiar caufe of any
fenfation or change in our turn of mind,
fo long as we are unacquainted with the
nature of the principles of fuch effects.
We neither know the way in which our
fpirits act, nor the manner of God's proceedings fo thoroughly, as in all cafes properly to diftinguifh them, and clearly to
explain them. We fhall, however, avoid
many miftakes; we fhall rightly judge of
our moral ftate, and uncommonly facilitate
the practice of religion, if we obferve the
remarks and examples I fhall now lay before you.

In

In the firft place, we are not to take every good defire or emotion we feel for the particular act of the Holy Ghoft. God is, indeed, all in all. His influence created every thing we behold; and we have to thank him for our exiftence, and the prefervation of our lives. His Providence extends no lefs over fpirits than over bodies. He maintains the powers of our fouls according to his Mighty Will; he elevates and ftrengthens them when and how he pleafes. Our dependance is intirely on him, and without him we can do nothing. But God acts not without means, where ordinary means are fufficient to his purpofe; he performs no miracle without a weighty caufe. He acts with us as with rational beings: he will have us to ufe the capacities he has given us; not dealing with us as with machines, which require continually to be pufhed on, or to be wound up for reaching their proper effect. He, therefore, that takes every lively thought,

thought, every acuter feeling excited in a delicate mind by reflecting on some important truth, for the confequences of an immediate influence of God, he plainly declares thereby that he underftands not the nature of the human foul, that he is accuftomed to make incomprehenfible myfteries of things that are to be deduced from natural caufes, and that he is poffeffed by fanatical principles. We muft, indeed, as I have already remarked, attribute all that we think or do to God, as the Father of lights, from whom all good gifts originally proceed ; but we do no honour to the Holy Ghoft, we render our piety fufpected, and make religion itfelf contemptible, when we afcribe to its operations all the emotions of our hearts, which are not unfrequently inordinate and impure enough. This erroneous opinion hath already given occafion to many abufes among chriftians. They that fuffer themfelves to be blinded thereby, generally hold their penetration;

their

their undertakings, and their actions, to be much greater and more important than indeed they are ; and it is by no means uncommon for such people to attribute to themselves a certain kind of infallibility ; at least, it is with difficulty they can be brought to endure contradiction. They imagine it to be impoffible for them to miftake, when they follow their inward impulfes; and the fingle affertion, *It is fo with me*, ftands them in ftead of all ground for their opinions.

In the fecond place, we muft carefully diftinguifh between the influence our natural conftitution, and our outward circumftances, have upon our exercifes of piety, and our moral conduct, from the operations of religion and the Spirit of God, and not take them for fpiritual experiences of a peculiar order. You know, Sirs, that our foul is moft intimately connected with our body ; and that no confiderable alteration

can happen to the one, but a correfpondent
alteration is to be perceived in the other.
When every part of our body is in health,
when the mixture and motion of its juices
go properly on, when we feel neither pain
nor languor, then our fpirit is alert and
active in all its functions; it operates freely, and without impediment, and it cofts
us no trouble to think with order and pre-
cifion. Reafon, then, prevails over all the
inferior powers of our foul, and we contemplate the truth in an unclouded light,
if no violent paffions intervene. But, on
the other hand, if ordinary or extraordinary alterations arife in our body, our underftanding and our foul no longer act in
fo regular a manner as they were hitherto
accuftomed to do. For inftance, if our
mind be affected by agreeable objects; if
we find ourfelves in a delightful country,
where nature prefents herfelf in all her
charms, and every living creature appears
to rejoice; if our heart be affected by the

6   tender

tender melody of founds; then our juices take a quicker motion; we are transported with joy, our thoughts flow on in a more rapid succession, and with increasing vivacity and vigour; and, if we then reflect on the sublime doctrines of religion, the pleasure we feel in them must of necessity be uncommonly great, they must often be perfectly extatic. On the other hand, when our body is attacked by any disorder; when the juices get thick, and the blood creeps heavily and flowly along in the veins; when the nerves become relaxed and feeble, the operations of our foul will be affected by the change. We shall find it laborious to think with order and continuity; our thoughts flowly succeed each other, with repeated interruptions; they will always have something obscure about them, and we shall endeavour in vain to render our comprehension fo active and clear as at other times. The moft important, the fublimeft truths, will then make but little

im-

impreffion on us. We may hear or read
the moft evident propofitions, and yet be
indifferent and almoft infenfible to them.
We fhall flee from joy, and fall an eafy
prey to prevailing fadnefs. The fame
thing may, in many refpects, be advanced
of the outward circumftances in which we
are placed. When we lead an unfollicitous,
a convenient, and a tranquil life; when we
can enjoy the delights of friendfhip, and
the agreeable converfation of a well-culti-
vated acquaintance, our thoughts will certainly flow more freely, our feelings will
be more lively, and we fhall confider and
practife religion with greater chearfulnefs
and ardour, than when we are oppreffed
by cares for food and raiment; when we
are in low and adverfe circumftances, when
one misfortune lays fiege to us after another; or when we are furrounded by de-
fponding perfons, and are obliged chiefly
to frequent the melancholy. So great is
the influence our conftitution and our outward

ward circumftances have on the offices and
operations of our foul. May we not, then,
be liable to miftake, when we reprefent
thefe alterations which fo naturally arife,
and are fo eafily explained, as fupernatural
revelations and particular interpofitions of
heaven? May we not deceive ourfelves,
when we efteem any more fenfible reflections, any more joyous fenfation, for immediate confolations from on high, or for the
raptures of heavenly tranfports? May we
not be vexed and tormented, in vain, when
we confider the indifference and comfort-
leffnefs which take their rife in the decays
of the body as a dereliction of God, or as
the tokens of his difpleafure, and indications of his wrath?

Neither are we, in the third place, to
reckon a certain particular degree of viva-
cioufnefs of fentiment as an effential part
of fpiritual experience. This is a very
hurtful prejudice of many chriftians, whom,

Y 3

how-

however, we cannot deny to have a sincere affection for virtue. They have a high eftimation of fenfible and violent feelings, and think their private acts of devotion cannot be acceptable without them. Their forrow for fin muft be accompanied by burning tears; their joy in God and his falvation muft be rapturous and extatic; their afpirations after eternal felicity muft be violent and tranfporting, or they think them of no advantage to their fpiritual concerns; a rational abftinence from every thing that is bad, a practical hatred againft it, a liberal and confiderate defign of uniformly acting in the fervice of God and goodnefs, a calm reliance on the perfections and wife providence of the Moft High, an immovable expectation of the kingdom of reafon and virtue to come, is by no means fufficient for them. Their blood muft have as great a fhare in their devotion as their rational fpirit, and perhaps a greater, for making them fatisfied with it. How much

ufe.

ufelefs pains do fuch perfons often take for
rouzing within them fome fenfible and vehement fenfation ! What difquietude, what
perturbation, what defpondency, are they
in, when they cannot raife their raptures to
the height they wifh them to attain, and
which they often regard as indifpenfably
neceffary ! Many a chriftian, with more
finccrity than judgement, falls to prayer in
his folitude; he humbles himfelf before
God for his manifold fins, confeffes the
unrighteoufnefs and infamy of his treafons,
abhors his failings and tranfgreffions, and
calls upon his God for compaffion and
pardon. Sin is, above all things, grievous
to him ; he wifhes for nothing fo much as
to be freed and purified from it ; he forms
the moft earneft intentions never more to
obey his irregular defires, but to live a life
of righteoufnefs and piety ; he devotes
himfelf, with all his heart, to a willing
and faithful obedience to all the commands
of God. In this manner he has a rational

and

and juft experience of the efficacy the doctrines of religion, poffefs of rendering their confeffors repentant, and of defending them from wickednefs and fin; and he has a right to reft upon them, and ftrenuoufly to fet about reducing his good refolutions to practice. But he is too much accuftomed to fenfitive reprefentations and feelings to be fatisfied with them. During his prayer he has felt no violent anguifh on account of his fins; he has had no feeling of the horrors of hell; his tears would not flow fo copioufly as he could have wifhed; his affurance of grace was not quite fo fenfible, and did not move him fo forcibly, as in other circumftances, and at other times. Thefe things fill him with diftruft; he laments over his hard and infenfible heart; he bewails his deplorable derelic-tion of God; he reprobates the imperfec-tion of his devotion, and imagines that God has turned away his face from him, and that he is utterly forfaken of heaven.

Thefe

These reflections plunge him into the deepeft difquietudes, and render the good effects which religion had operated in him, at leaft for a length of time, intirely fruitlefs. Trouble and tormenting follicitudes take poffeffion of his foul; and nothing will reftore him to tranquillity and peace till he be able to call forth thofe tears, and excite thofe fenfible emotions, thofe violent feelings, which he has hitherto endeavoured in vain to produce. Then, for the firft time, he experiences, according to his idea, the bitternefs of fin; then taftes. peace with God, feels a confidence of forgivenefs, and then feems to hear the Moft High calling out to him, "Thy fins are forgiven thee."—But, how liable to error is fuch a conduct as this! Does religion, then, confift in thefe fenfual feelings, in a more rapid or more fluggifh circulation of the blood and the animal fpirits? or in the plain and juft defign, the firm and ftedfaft refolution, and the earneft endeavour to

walk

walk after its precepts? Are we not to
worſhip God in ſpirit and in truth? Is not
the chriſtian worſhip a reaſonable ſervice?
Muſt we found our tranquillity, our comfort, and our hopes, on things that are not
in our power, which depend on the changeable conſtitution of our bodies, on the degree of our health, our outward circumſtances, and frequently even on accidents?
Are we to make the diſcharge of our duties
unneceſſarily oppreſſive and hard, and
thereby hinder our progreſs in virtue? Are
we to live in a conſtant turmoil and confuſion, and never enjoy the pleaſing tranquillity which true virtue provides for her
friends? No. The more rational, gentle,
and quiet our experiences of the power of
religion be, the leſs ſenſible and eventual
they are, the better and more infallible
are they.

Fourthly, we muſt neither lay down our
own experiences and feelings as a law for
others,

others, nor make foreign experiences and
feelings a law to ourfelves. The effects
which the doctrines of religion produce in
different men, are, as we have already no-
ticed, as various as their temperaments,
their fagacity, and other circumftances;
indeed, not effentially, but yet in quality
and degree. With one perfon they are
more lively and fenfual; with another,
more rational and fpiritual. Many have
received from nature a foft and tender
heart, and are moved on all occafions in
the moft fenfible manner; their mind and
their imagination are ever alert and bufy.
They have an influence on all their actions.
Do they confider their failings and fins?
Sorrow pervades their foul, and burfts
from their eyes in a torrent of tears. Do
they reprefent to themfelves the grace of
God, the love of the Redeemer, or the
happinefs of heaven? they are loft in the
moft pleafing admiration, and their joy
proceeds to extafy. But, are not fuch
chrif-

chriftians deceived, when they imagine that
the degree of forrow, or of joy, to which
they attain, is a general and effential token
of true chriflianity? Are they not over-
hafty in their judgement, when they reckon
all for unconverted and vicious men, who,
in thefe refpects, cannot do the like? We
muft therefore never conclude, from what
we feel and experience, that all fincere
worfhipers of God and Chrift ought to
feel in the fame manner and the fame degree. No more muft we take the experiences of others for the unqualified model
of our imitation. Many a fincere chriftian,
by not attending to this rule, has embar-
raffed himfelf in the greateft difficulties.
He reads, or he hears, that this or the
other faint, in his penitence, fell into an
uncommon and continued forrow; that he
felt an extraordinary remorfe, and for a
long time was inconfolably afflicted, and,
day and night, lamented and bewailed his
fins—and the like. From want of knowledge,

ledge, he conceives this to be a neceſſary part of real repentance, and that he muſt experience the very ſame before he can properly ſay he is converted. Accordingly he torments himſelf ſo long, till he thinks he is come up to the pattern before him; let his nature and conſtitution oppoſe itſelf as ſtrongly as it may. But can ſuch violent and unnatural feelings deſerve the name of ſpiritual and godly experiences of the power of religion? Can you poſſibly imagine, Sirs, that theſe agitations can be agreeable to the Creator of our frame, who requires of us a voluntary worſhip and a rational obedience? Certainly not. He has, indeed, patience with theſe infirmities; but they are contrary to his deſigns, in oppoſition to his will, and can only tend to the prejudice of him that entertains them.

Laſtly, in theſe ſpiritual experiences we muſt never forget the enlightening of our mind, and the uſe of our reaſon. This

i₃

is a common fault with numbers of chriſtians. They are ſo much employed in exciting ſenſual ſenſations in themſelves, and in obtaining what they often falſely term ſpiritual experience, that they give themſelves little or no concern about cultivating the nobler part of their being, their rational ſpirit, and bringing it to a higher degree of perfection. They prefer the violent ebullitions of their blood to the tranquil operations of reaſon, and ſeem to be all ſenſation. Their knowledge is, therefore, generally very obſcure and imperfect; they regard the augmentation and improvement of it as merely a bye-work of little importance. Their feelings compenſate the injuries of ignorance and error: they think ſentiment the ſafeſt guide. Nay, they go ſo far as to ſcorn the ſuggeſtions of reaſon, and take all poſſible care not to make uſe of her precepts, or follow her light. Such diſpoſitions naturally lead to fanaticiſm, and to all the extravagances attend-

attendant on it. So foon as we neglect the ufe of reafon, we are immediately in danger of being deceived and feduced by our own hearts. Experience and fancy may be eafily confounded in a warm imagination : how are we to difcriminate them from each other, unlefs we are guided in our judgement by an enlightened and a trained underftanding ? And what is all our religion and virtue, if it be not founded on knowledge and certainty ? Can we emancipate ourfelves from the bonds of fuperftition, if we act not from argument, but merely from impulfe ? Indeed, the more clear our knowledge is, the more juftly and folidly we accuftom ourfelves to think ; fo much the more gentle and orderly will our emotions be, fo much the more rational and confiftent our fpiritual experiences. But, even this brings us nearer to perfection ; it gives our worfhip and our virtue a real value ; it renders our conduct harmonious, and fits us thereby, by degrees, for that

pure

pure and exalted devotion in which the
inhabitants of heaven are employed.

These, Sirs, are the principal rules we
must observe, in regard to spiritual experiences, if we would be safe from the ex-
travagancies of superstition, and the follies
of fanaticism.

You will much mistake my meaning,
however, if you draw from it this false
conclusion; that all that is hereby said of
spiritual experience rests on the imagination alone, and that the bare knowledge
of religion is sufficient to salvation. No.
No one can be a true christian, who does
not confess and experience the godly influence of the doctrines of Jesus, and difplay the fruit of them in his whole deportment. Your knowledge, christians, must
be lively and active; you must moderate
your affection for earthly things; you must
purify your hearts, and direct your inclinations

tions to worthy objects; you muſt reform, regenerate, and amend, and regulate every part of your conduct, if you would be happy. Try yourſelves by theſe marks, and reſt not in the outward privileges and tokens of chriſtians. If you can reflect upon ſin without hatred and abhorrence, on goodneſs and virtue without eſteem and love; on the favour of God, and the example of Jeſus, without admiration and gratitude; and the bliſs of heaven, without aſpirations after it; if all theſe have but a feeble or no influence at all on your reſolutions and actions, you are then of the number of thoſe hypocrites who deny by their works what they confeſs in their words.—Would you avoid the dreadful lot, which, as ſuch, you muſt expect for eternity, expand your hearts to the ſalutary effects of the religion of Jeſus. Let the doctrines it teaches us be powerful in you. Follow their ſuggeſtions, and teſtify the integrity of your faith by an unremit-

VOL. II. Z ted

ted ardour in all good works. Call upon God for his powerful affiftance in thefe arduous endeavours, and beware of grieving the fpirit of grace by pertinacious oppofition. Thus will you know, as our Saviour declares, that his doctrine is from God. You will remember that it has the power to render its fincere. followers virtuous, holy, tranquil, chearful, and happy ; that it will fupport you in all trials, and comfort you in all afflictions ; that it will not leave you even in the fhades of death ; and that you will thereby obtain the actual pof. feffion of that vaft felicity it affures us of.

END OF THE SECOND VOLUME.